PRAYING UP YOUR

YOUR

leading

MAN

Paperback ISBN: 978-1-967262-01-4

A Publication of *H22 Productions*

| 1 25 25 20 16 02 |

Published in the United States of America

PRAYING UP YOUR
leading
MAN

EMPOWERING YOUR HUSBAND THROUGH PRAYER

—— A 20 DAY DEVOTIONAL ——

SUSAN HALAUT

h22
PRODUCTIONS

Endorsements

"This devotional is a beautiful invitation for women to partner with God through prayer—not pressure—as they support their husbands in becoming the leaders their families need. What makes Praying Up Your Leading Man so impactful is the way Susan weaves real-life storytelling into each devotional, grounding biblical truth in relatable, heartfelt experiences.

If you've ever felt alone in your desire for deeper connection, stronger spiritual leadership, or a more unified marriage, this book will meet you right where you are—with grace, encouragement, and a whole lot of hope."

—April Adams Pertuis,
Founder of Lightbeamers & Visibility +
Storytelling Coach

"Praying Up Your Leading Man is beautifully poignant - a must-read for every woman of faith. The reflections and calls to action bring the devotions to life. This book promises to change the game for Christian marriages and families!"

—Judy Weber
Judy Weber, Esq.
Business Strategist & Coach

"Susan Halaut's Praying Up Your Leading Man is a powerful, faith-filled journey that every wife should experience. This book guided me through 20 days of purposeful prayer, helping me see my husband through God's eyes—as a leader, a partner, and a man called to greatness.

Susan's heartfelt stories showed me how my prayers can build up my husband in every area, from his faith to our intimacy. Her wisdom and grace make this devotional a beacon of hope, inspiring me to partner with God in strengthening our marriage. Susan, your passion for equipping wives to pray boldly is a blessing, and this book will ignite a spark in countless homes!"

—Tonya Telesco
Inspirational Speaker | Author | Leadership Expert
Faculty Member at Global John Maxwell Team

"Few books have the power to truly transform marriages—this is one of them. Praying Up Your Leading Man is a call to action for wives to rise up as prayer warriors, not worriers. Susan combines heart, humor, and holy boldness to show us that prayer isn't passive—it's powerful. Every devotional will inspire you to speak life over your husband, your marriage, and your future together. If you're ready to stop striving and start inviting God to lead your relationship, this book is your guide."

—Greg & Julie Gorman
Founders of Married for a Purpose
Authors, Speakers, Marriage Coaches

Acknowledgments

To my husband, Jeff — my protector, encourager, best friend, life partner, and lover. I honestly don't have words big enough for the gratitude I feel. Your steady presence and quiet strength have anchored me through every high and low. Thank you for believing in this book, and even more, for believing in me. I love doing life with you ... especially now that I've matured into the kind of wife who doesn't regularly make you consider sleeping on the rooftop. (Proverbs 21:9, anyone?)

To Jeffrey, Spencer, Andrew, and Cameron — "the boys." While I only birthed one of you, God gave me the gift of all four of you. Each of you has shaped me. You've sharpened me, softened me, stretched me, and grown me. God has used your lives to transform mine — molding me into a woman who is more compassionate, more present, and (thankfully) a little less dramatic than the one you grew up with. I love you deeply, and I'm grateful for the journey we've shared.

To my son, Cameron — walking beside you on your journey of recovery has changed my prayer life forever. It taught me how to surrender in the hardest way: by praying not for comfort, but for rock bottom — because I knew that's where Jesus would meet you. That is one of the hardest prayers I've ever prayed. But God was faithful. God is faithful. And I'm honored to witness His work in your life.

To the Holy Spirit — thank You for entrusting me with this message. For whispering truth when I doubted, for prompting me to keep writing when I wanted to stop, and for flooding my heart with stories that reminded me this was never just about my words. May this devotional point wives back to You — the One who empowers, equips, and intercedes when we don't know what to pray.

To Nick Poe and the amazing team at H22 Publishing — thank you for making my first publishing experience such a joy. The process was smooth, efficient, and full of kindness. Your quick communication, thoughtful edits, and professional guidance made this book feel well-loved before it ever reached the hands of a reader.

To Greg and Julie Gorman, founders of Married For A Purpose and H22 Publishing — thank you for believing in this message and for creating a space where biblically grounded truth meets practical, Spirit-led purpose. Your mentorship and mission inspire me.

And finally, to you — the reader. The wife. The prayer warrior. The woman who wants to see her husband walk in the fullness of God's calling. Thank you for trusting me with your time and your heart. I've prayed for you on every page.

"The wise woman builds her house, but with her own hands the foolish one tears hers down."

Proverbs 14:1 (NIV)

Here's to being the kind of women who build — with prayer, with purpose, and with hope.

Contents

Introduction

WHY PRAYING FOR OUR HUSBANDS MATTERS

In countless conversations with Christian women, both in-person and online, I hear the same heartfelt cry: "How do I encourage my husband to lead our home?" Many wives feel a deep desire for godly leadership from their husbands—leadership rooted in love, strength, and integrity. These women feel the weight of filling a role they believe is meant for their husbands and wonder, "What do I do when I know leadership isn't my God-given role, but someone has to do it?" The longing for spiritual partnership in marriage is real and powerful, and many women feel they are carrying a burden not meant for them alone.

Yet, the path to encouraging godly leadership in our homes is not always clear. Culture sends mixed messages about men, masculinity, and leadership. We live in a world quick to point fingers at "toxic masculinity" and to celebrate female independence, often implying that men's leadership is outdated or undesirable. This message has left many men uncertain about their role, unsure of what's expected of them, and questioning their worth and purpose. Some become discouraged or complacent, thinking, "Why try if I'm only going to be criticized?"

Adding to this challenge is the increasing prevalence of broken families. With rising divorce rates, many young men grow up without their fathers or any compassionate, godly male role model in their lives. When boys lack a father figure to demonstrate humble strength, kindness, and spiritual leadership, it's hard for them to develop those qualities themselves. As a result, many young men reach adulthood feeling ill-prepared to lead their own families, unsure of how to model something they've never seen.

As wives, we may feel stuck—desiring our husbands to take on a godly leadership role but unsure how to support and encourage that in a way that respects, loves, and builds him up. Our hearts ache for homes where husbands and wives share a partnership rooted in Christ, where husbands confidently lead and serve with love, and where wives feel secure, valued, and cherished. But how do we get there?

This devotional, Praying Up Your Leading Man, was born out of this desire to empower wives to pray over the unique and vital aspects of our husbands' lives and roles. Each day, we'll dive into specific prayers that can lift our husbands up, support their growth in godly leadership, and help them feel equipped to step into their role with courage and faith. We'll cover topics that shape a godly leader, from finances to character, from friendships to fatherhood, from courage to the vital influence of the Holy Spirit. Through each day's reflection, we can be intentional in prayer, asking God to work in their hearts, minds, and lives—and to shape us as their partners along the way.

As we pray, we become allies in our husbands' journey toward godly leadership. We're not competing or controlling; we're supporting and encouraging. In this way, prayer becomes a powerful act of love, sowing seeds of faith, trust, and strength that can bear fruit in our marriages and families for generations to come. This is our chance to lift up our husbands, to lean into God's design for marriage, and to experience the joy of seeing our prayers at work in the men we love.

So, let's begin this journey together, day by day, praying up our leading men and trusting God to lead them—and us—through.

Day 1

LEADERSHIP

"For the husband is the head of the wife as Christ is the head of the church..."

Sarah and John had been married for nearly a decade. Sarah was a natural leader—organized, detail-oriented, and quick to make decisions, especially when running their household. With two young children and both of them working, life was busy, and the responsibilities often felt overwhelming. Over time, Sarah found herself handling almost everything: managing the finances, making decisions for the kids, scheduling appointments, and coordinating family activities. On the other hand, John was quieter and often took a backseat in these areas. Sarah loved him deeply, but she wished he would step up as the leader in their home, especially in spiritual matters.

Sarah tried to lead gently, hoping her example might inspire John to take more initiative. But as months passed, she began to feel more burdened. Sarah would round up the kids every Sunday morning, get everyone ready for church, and sometimes even drive them there while John trailed along. She didn't resent him; she just felt exhausted and alone in the responsibility. She had even tried to initiate family devotions, but John usually stayed silent or deferred to her to lead the prayers. Sometimes, he seemed utterly disinterested altogether.

One particularly exhausting Sunday, Sarah found herself feeling both frustrated and sad. She didn't want to nag John or make him feel inadequate, but she longed to see him take on the spiritual leadership she believed God intended for him to step into. That evening, after the kids were in bed, she poured her heart out to God, praying, "Lord, please show John the value and importance of leading our family in faith. I know it's not my role to push or pressure him, but I need help. I want to feel supported and for our kids to see their dad as a spiritual leader."

Days went by, and Sarah continued to pray, choosing to release her desires to God and letting go of her attempts to take control. A few weeks later, on a quiet Saturday morning, John approached her. "Hey, I was thinking," he said with a hesitant smile. "Maybe on Sundays, before we go to church, we could set aside a little time for the family to pray together or go over a Bible story with the kids." Sarah's heart nearly skipped a beat. She tried to hide her surprise and excitement, giving a gentle nod. "I'd love that," she said, keeping her response simple and supportive, resisting the urge to make too many suggestions.

The following Sunday, after breakfast, John gathered everyone in the living room. Sarah watched as he brought out a simple devotional he'd found online, guided their family in a short reading, and then led them in prayer. His voice was steady but soft, and she could tell he was nervous. The kids fidgeted, only half-paying attention, but Sarah could barely contain her gratitude. John was doing it. He was stepping into the role she had prayed for, which was beautiful in its simplicity.

Over the next few weeks, this new routine became a cherished family time. Each Sunday, John grew a bit more comfortable, and he even started adding in his thoughts and asking the kids questions about the Bible stories they were reading. Sarah saw the kids beginning to look to him as a spiritual guide, something she had longed for. She felt lighter, less alone in her responsibility, and more like they were partners. Watching John grow into this role reminded her that prayer, patience, and gentle encouragement had a much more profound effect than any amount of nagging or pushing.

For Sarah, this journey was about seeing her husband take on leadership and about learning to trust God with the things she couldn't control.

"For the husband is the head of the wife as Christ is the head of the church, his body, of which he is the Savior." – Ephesians 5:23 (NIV)

This verse lays the foundation for God's design for marriage, emphasizing the husband's role as the spiritual leader of the home. However, it is crucial to understand that this leadership mirrors Christ's example, characterized by sacrificial love, humility, and a commitment to nurture and protect. Just as Christ leads the church with grace and selflessness, husbands are called to lead their families in a way that reflects God's love and brings spiritual strength to the home.

> **Your prayers can pave the way for his growth without pressuring him.**

John's reluctance to lead reflects a common challenge in many marriages, where societal expectations or personal insecurities make husbands hesitate to embrace their God-given role. This verse encourages husbands like John to view leadership not as dominance or control but as a loving responsibility to guide their families closer to God. When John takes the step to lead family devotions, he exemplifies the type of Christ-like leadership that fosters unity and spiritual growth in the home.

For wives, this verse reminds them of the importance of supporting and encouraging their husbands in their leadership roles. Sarah's approach of gentle encouragement and prayer is a model for helping her husband step into his God-ordained role without pressure or criticism. Her faithfulness reflects her trust that God can equip and empower her husband to lead well.

Some husbands may readily embrace leadership, while others may feel hesitant or unsure. If your husband is resistant or unaware of his role, trust that God's timing and work in his heart are perfect. Your prayers can pave the way for his growth without pressuring him.

This verse applies to all Christian homes. Husbands are called to lead their families with the same love, humility, and self-sacrifice that Christ shows the church. This leadership includes spiritual guidance, fostering emotional and physical safety, and making decisions that honor God. For wives, the call is to support, respect, and pray for their husbands as they navigate this responsibility.

Ultimately, this verse reminds us that godly leadership is not about power or control—it's about service, love, and a commitment to building a home where Christ is at the center. When husbands lead as Christ leads the church, and wives come alongside them in support, the marriage becomes a reflection of God's design, bringing glory to Him and creating a strong foundation for the family.

REFLECTION:

1. Do I encourage my husband's leadership, or do I sometimes try to take over?

What underlying fears or past experiences might influence my tendency to take control? In what specific ways can I encourage my husband's leadership while trusting him and God?

2. How am I expecting my husband to show up in the leadership role of our family?

Am I seeking God's guidance for my husband's leadership role, or are my expectations shaped by personal desires or societal standards? How often do I pray for God to reveal His specific plan for my husband's leadership in our family?

3. How do I respond to my husband's leadership role?

How do I respond when my husband's leadership looks different from what I envisioned? Am I encouraging him or comparing him to others? Am I trusting God's timing and process for developing my husband's leadership, or am I impatiently trying to control the outcome?

PRAYER:

"Lord, thank you for the role you've given my husband in our home. I pray for his heart and mind to be rooted in your wisdom as he leads us. Help me to respect and support his leadership. Give him strength to follow Your example, leading with humility and love. Amen."

TODAY'S CALL TO ACTION:

Write a note or verbally express gratitude to your husband for a specific way he has shown leadership in your home, no matter how big or small. Pray specifically for one area where he can grow in leadership.

Day 2

LEAVING & CLEAVING

"A man shall leave his father and mother and hold fast to his wife..."

J en and Mark were newlyweds, only six months into their marriage, but they were already finding that the transition into married life wasn't as smooth as they'd imagined. Jen loved Mark's family—they were warm and welcoming and had embraced her as one of their own from the start. But she also noticed something that quietly nagged at her heart: Mark's mom was a little too involved in their lives. She called Mark daily, sometimes multiple times a day, asking his advice on everything from fixing the Wi-Fi to how to handle disagreements with his dad.

At first, Jen tried to shrug it off. Mark was close to his mom, which wasn't bad. But over time, she began to feel like their marriage wasn't truly theirs. Instead of making decisions together, it often felt like Mark was running things by his mom first. When they were out on dates or just relaxing at home, the constant phone calls from his mom started to feel intrusive. One evening, as they were finishing dinner, his phone buzzed again, and Jen couldn't hide her disappointment. "It's my mom," Mark said, glancing at the screen and reaching to answer. Jen sighed softly, hoping he'd notice, but he didn't.

That night, Jen felt torn. She loved Mark deeply and didn't want to come between him and his family, but she also felt as if she wasn't his priority. She prayed, asking God for wisdom and the right words to express her feelings without causing a rift. The next morning, as they sat together drinking coffee, Jen took a deep breath. "Mark, can I share something with you?" she asked gently. He nodded, looking up from his phone. "I love how close you are to your mom. It's one of the things I admire about you. But sometimes, I feel like we're not getting enough space to build our relationship. I want us to be the ones who make decisions about our life together." She paused, hoping he wouldn't take it the wrong way. "What do you think?"

Mark frowned, his expression conflicted. "I don't want to hurt her feelings," he said after a long pause. "She's always counted on me, even before we got married. I don't want her to feel abandoned." Jen nodded, understanding his struggle. "I know you don't want to hurt her. And I'm not asking you to pull away from her entirely. I just think there's a balance, and

I'd love to figure it out together." Mark was quiet, but he promised to think about it.

Over the next few days, Jen noticed Mark trying to create some boundaries. He started letting some of his mom's calls go to voicemail and talked with her less about the personal details of their marriage. A week later, Mark sat down with his mom for a heart-to-heart conversation. "Mom, I love you and am always here for you," he began. "But now that I'm married to Jen, I need to make sure she's my priority. That doesn't mean I love you any less. It just means I want to make sure my marriage starts on the right foot." His mom looked hurt at first but then nodded slowly. "I understand," she said. "It's just hard to let go."

Mark reassured her that their relationship would remain strong, but he needed her to trust him to lead his new family. As he shared this with Jen later, she felt a wave of gratitude. It wasn't easy for Mark, but he stepped up in a way that showed he valued her and their marriage.

Over time, the boundaries they set became a natural part of their lives. Jen noticed that his confidence as a husband grew as Mark focused more on their relationship. She felt secure, knowing that their marriage was becoming the priority it was meant to be. And Mark's mom, though initially hesitant, adjusted to the new dynamic, building a healthier relationship with them both.

This experience reminded Jen that building a godly marriage takes intentionality, courage, and sometimes diffi-cult conversations. It also reinforced the importance of prayer—trusting God to work in her husband's heart instead of trying to control the situation herself. Through this, Jen and Mark began to truly "leave and cleave," laying a strong foundation for the life they were building together.

For couples in stepfamilies, leaving and cleaving becomes even more essential, as it often involves breaking emotional or obligatory ties to an ex-spouse. While co-parenting may require some ongoing interaction, it's crucial to establish healthy boundaries that prioritize your current marriage. Emotional dependency, unresolved tensions, or frequent involvement in your ex's personal matters can create stress and insecurity in your new relationship.

Mark and Jen's story reminds us that true unity requires both partners to fully commit to each other, leaving behind old patterns that no longer serve the new marriage. In a stepfamily, this may mean intentionally shifting your focus from the past to the future you're building together. By communicating openly, setting boundaries, and seeking God's guidance, couples can ensure that their marriage remains the primary relationship, creating a foundation of trust and peace for their blended family.

"A man shall leave his father and mother and hold fast to his wife, and they shall become one flesh." – Genesis 2:24 (NIV)

This foundational verse for marriage emphasizes the importance of prioritizing the marital relationship above all other earthly relationships. Leaving and cleaving is not merely about physical separation from parents but creating a new, independent unit where the husband and wife are united. This unity requires emotional, spiritual, and relational shifts that enable the couple to fully invest in building a strong and lasting partnership.

In the story, Mark's struggle to set boundaries with his mother highlights the challenges many couples face in honoring this principle. While love and respect for parents remain essential, this verse teaches that loyalty and focus must shift to one's spouse. Mark's decision to establish healthy boundaries and prioritize Jen demonstrates obedience to this biblical design, strengthening their trust and fostering oneness in their marriage.

> " Leaving and cleaving is not merely about physical separation from parents but creating a new, independent unit where the husband and wife are united.

This verse has additional significance for stepfamilies. It calls couples to leave behind emotional entanglements with past relationships, including ex-spouses, to invest in their current marriage fully. While co-parenting responsibilities may persist, this principle requires that the new marriage take precedence, setting a clear foundation for unity and trust within the blended family. Investing in a marriage coach or counselor specializing in blended family dynamics can be incredibly beneficial.

This verse applies to all married couples, calling us to examine any relationships or obligations that might hinder our oneness. These could include unhealthy parental ties, over-reliance on friends, or unresolved attachments to past relationships. Cleaving to one's spouse involves physical closeness and a deep commitment to protect, nurture, and prioritize the marital bond.

For husbands and wives, this verse is a reminder that marriage is a sacred covenant designed by God to reflect unity and mutual dependence. When couples leave behind old patterns and focus on holding fast to one another, they create a strong foundation for their marriage rooted in love and trust. By living out this principle, couples honor God's design for marriage and experience the blessings of unity and partnership.

REFLECTION:

1. Are there relationships or habits that distract us from prioritizing each other?

What specific relationships or habits might still draw my husband or me away from fully cleaving to each other? How can I lovingly address these distractions and seek God's wisdom in creating healthy boundaries?

2. How can I encourage my husband to keep our marriage first without feeling pressured?

Am I creating a safe space for my husband to express his

feelings about outside influences on our marriage? How can I approach this conversation with grace, seeking unity rather than control?

3. What boundaries can we establish to keep our marriage strong and unified?

Are there practical steps we can take as a couple to protect the sanctity of our marriage? How can I prayerfully support my husband in navigating difficult or sensitive relationships?

PRAYER:

"Father, I thank you for our marriage and the bond we share. Help us both to prioritize each other above all earthly ties, and to keep our relationship first after you. Give my husband courage to leave behind any past loyalties that pull him from our oneness. Make us inseparable in your love. Amen."

TODAY'S CALL TO ACTION:

Identify one relationship or habit that may be pulling focus away from your marriage. Commit to praying about it and discussing with your husband how to set healthy boundaries to protect your unity.

Day 3

FINANCES

"And my God will meet all your needs..."

B eth and Mike had always tried to be careful with their money, but life had a way of throwing unexpected challenges their way. Between car repairs, medical bills, and the rising cost of groceries, it felt like their budget was always stretched to its breaking point. Beth, a planner by nature, loved spreadsheets and carefully tracking every dollar. Mike, on the other hand, was more relaxed about finances. He believed in saving when they could but also in enjoying life. This difference in approach often led to tension, especially during tight months.

One evening, Beth sat at the kitchen table, her laptop open and her head in her hands. The numbers just weren't adding up. They were dipping into their savings again, and she didn't see how they could avoid it. Mike walked in, saw her distress, and asked, "What's wrong?" Beth let out a long sigh. "I'm trying to make this budget work, but we're going to run out of savings if something doesn't change. I feel like I'm carrying all this responsibility, and it's exhausting."

Mike frowned, feeling a mix of guilt and helplessness. "I didn't realize it was weighing on you this much," he admitted. "I guess I've just trusted you to handle it because you're so good at it." Beth looked up, her frustration softening. "I don't want to do this alone," she said quietly. "I need us to tackle this together."

After putting the kids to bed that night, Beth and Mike sat down with their budget. They went through everything together for the first time in a long time—income, expenses, and goals. As they talked, Beth realized how much Mike valued experiences, like taking the kids to the zoo or going out for ice cream as a family, even if it meant spending a little extra. Mike, in turn, saw how much Beth valued security and wanted to ensure they were prepared for emergencies. It was a moment of understanding that neither of them had expected.

As they wrapped up their discussion, Mike suggested something that caught Beth off guard: "Why don't we pray about this? I know we're doing everything we possible, but maybe we need to ask God for wisdom and trust Him to provide." Beth nodded, and for the first time in their marriage, they prayed specifically about their finances.

Mike's prayer was simple but heartfelt, asking God to give them wisdom, unity, and peace as they worked together to manage what He had given them.

Over the next few months, their financial situation didn't change dramatically, but their approach did. They started having regular budget meetings, where they discussed not only numbers but also their priorities and how they could align their spending with their values. They learned to compromise—Beth relaxed her strict rules a little to allow for the occasional treat, and Mike became more intentional about saving. They also began tithing consistently, something they had talked about for years but never fully committed to.

One day, out of the blue, Mike received a small bonus at work. It wasn't life-changing, but it covered an unexpected expense that had just popped up. Beth and Mike looked at each other and smiled, knowing it was God's provision. That moment reminded them that trusting God with their finances wasn't just about praying for help but inviting Him into the process and being faithful stewards of what they had.

The most significant change for Beth wasn't in their bank account but in their partnership. She no longer felt like she was carrying the burden alone, and Mike felt more invested in their family's financial well-being. Together, they experienced the peace that comes from aligning their hearts and resources with God's plan.

"And my God will meet all your needs according to the riches of his glory in Christ Jesus." –Philippians 4:19 (NIV)

This verse is a powerful reminder of God's provision and faithfulness. It assures believers that God will meet their needs—not necessarily all their wants, but everything they truly need—out of the abundance of His riches in Christ. It redirects our trust from earthly resources to God, the ultimate source of provision, reminding us that He is sovereign over all our circumstances, including financial ones.

> By keeping our eyes on God rather than our circumstances, we experience His provision and grow in faith, unity, and reliance on Him.

Beth and Mike's financial struggles highlight a situation many couples face—how to navigate seasons of scarcity or uncertainty. This verse speaks directly to their need for reassurance, reminding them that their security does not lie in their bank account but in God's limitless ability to provide. As they pray and seek God together, they align their hearts with His promises and experience His provision through practical opportunities and a deepened sense of peace.

The application of this verse calls couples to approach finances as a team, with faith at the center of their decisions. Instead of falling into fear or conflict, they are encouraged to trust God, seek His guidance, and steward their resources wisely. This might involve making sacrifices, budgeting with intention, or being generous even when it feels counterintuitive, trusting that God honors faithfulness.

It also challenges couples to distinguish between needs and desires. In a world that often equates success with material abundance, this verse reminds us to be content with what God provides, trusting that He knows and supplies what is truly best for us.

If you and your husband are not aligned on financial stewardship or if he struggles to take the initiative in this area, ask God for wisdom in how to navigate these challenges with grace. Trust that He will guide you in stewarding your resources faithfully.

For Beth and Mike (and all couples) this verse is a call to surrender our financial burdens to God and trust in His provision. Living with gratitude is also a challenge, acknowledging that every blessing comes from Him. By keeping our eyes on God rather than our circumstances, we experience His provision and grow in faith, unity, and reliance on Him. This trust transforms their financial struggles into opportunities to see God's faithfulness at work in their lives.

REFLECTION:

1. Do I trust God to provide for our needs, or do I worry about finances often?

What financial worries or past experiences might challenge

my trust in God's provision?? How can I pray for peace and surrender in this area? When has God provided in unexpected ways? What experiences can I use as a testimony to remind myself of God's faithfulness and provision?

2. How can I support my husband in making wise financial decisions?

Am I contributing to financial discussions in a way that encourages collaboration and trust? What practical ways can I support his leadership in this area while offering my perspective?

3. What areas of our spending or saving could we pray over together?

Are there patterns in our financial habits that we've overlooked or taken for granted? How can we make prayer a regular part of our financial planning to align our goals with God's will?

PRAYER:

"God, you are our provider, and I trust you with our finances. Please give my husband wisdom in managing our resources. Let our finances be a source of unity, not stress. Help us to be generous and responsible, always honoring you with what we have. Amen."

TODAY'S CALL TO ACTION:

Have a brief, honest conversation with your husband about one financial goal or concern. Pray together over your family's finances, asking God for wisdom and provision.

Day 4

EMOTIONS

"For God has not given us a spirit of fear..."

L aura had always known that her husband, James, wasn't the type to express his feelings openly. He was steady and dependable, the rock of their family. He had a quiet nature and rarely talked about what was on his mind. Lately, however, Laura had noticed a shift. James seemed more irritable and withdrawn, especially after coming home from work. The spark in his eyes had dimmed, and he seemed to snap at small things that never used to bother him.

One evening, James came home, tossed his bag on the floor, and went straight to their bedroom without a word. While cleaning up after dinner and their two kids playing in the living room, Laura felt her chest tighten. It wasn't the first time this had happened recently, and it was starting to weigh on her. She felt hurt and unsure of what to do. Should she confront him? Should she let it go? A hundred thoughts raced through her mind.

She decided to give him some space for the moment. Later that evening, after the kids were in bed, Laura went to the bedroom. James was sitting on the edge of the bed, his shoulders slumped, staring at the floor. Laura felt a nudge in her spirit to approach him gently. She sat down beside him without saying anything and rested her hand lightly on his arm. For a moment, the silence felt heavy, but she resisted the urge to fill it with words.

Finally, James let out a deep sigh. "I'm sorry," he said quietly, his voice thick with emotion. "I've been so short with you and the kids. It's not fair to any of you."

Laura felt a mix of relief and compassion. "Do you want to talk about it?" she asked softly.

At first, he didn't respond, and she wondered if she had overstepped. But then he began to speak, hesitantly at first, then with more openness. He explained that work had been overwhelming. His company was downsizing, and while his job was safe for now, he was carrying the weight of increased responsibilities and an unspoken fear about what the future might hold. "I feel like I have to keep it all together," he admitted. "But I don't know how much longer I can."

Laura listened intently, her heart breaking for him. She had seen the signs of his stress but hadn't realized how deeply it affected him. She fought back tears and whispered,

"You don't have to carry this alone. I'm here, and more importantly, God's here. Can I pray with you?"

James hesitated, then nodded. Laura reached for his hand, holding it tightly as she began to pray. Her words were simple but heartfelt: "Lord, you know the burden James is carrying. You see his heart and his worries. Please give him peace and remind him that he's not alone in this. Help him to lean on you and to know that it's okay to feel what he's feeling. Thank you for being our strength when we feel weak. Amen."

As she finished, she glanced at James and saw tears in his eyes. "Thank you," he said quietly, squeezing her hand. That moment of vulnerability brought them closer than they had felt in weeks. It reminded Laura of the power of listening without judgment and offering prayer instead of solutions.

Over the next few days, Laura noticed a subtle but steady shift in James. He started coming home a little earlier when he could, spending more time with her and the kids. He even initiated a few conversations about work, something he had rarely done before. Laura continued to pray for him daily, asking God to give him strength and peace. And James, feeling the support of his wife and the presence of God, began to open up more often, sharing both his worries and his joys.

This experience taught Laura the importance of creating a safe space for her husband to express his emotions. She realized that while she couldn't fix his struggles, she could be a source of comfort and encouragement, pointing him back to the One who could carry his burdens. And for James, it was a reminder that even the strongest men need a place to rest and be vulnerable—and that it's okay to lean on both God and the people who love you.

"For God has not given us a spirit of fear, but of power, and of love and of a sound mind." – 2 Timothy 1:7 (NKJV)

This verse reminds believers that God equips us with His Spirit, enabling us to overcome fear and navigate our emotions with strength, love, and discipline. It emphasizes that our emotional state does not have to be ruled by circumstances or insecurities, as God has given us the tools to respond to challenges in a way that reflects His peace and purpose.

> **Our emotional state does not have to be ruled by circumstances or insecurities, as God has given us the tools to respond to challenges in a way that reflects His peace and purpose.**

In the story, James's emotional exhaustion and struggle to open up to Laura reflect the common challenges of managing feelings like fear, frustration, or inadequacy. This verse speaks directly to his situation, assuring him that God's Spirit provides comfort and the power to face his emotions with courage and clarity. Laura's gentle encouragement and prayer further demonstrate how love and compassion can foster emotional healing and connection.

This verse applies to individuals and couples. It calls believers to recognize that emotions, while natural and valid, should not control us. Instead, we are invited to rely on the Spirit to respond with love and wisdom, even in moments of stress or conflict. This involves practicing self-control—pausing to pray, reflect, and seek God's perspective before reacting impulsively.

This verse encourages mutual support in navigating emotions for couples. Like Laura, one partner can offer grace and patience. At the same time, the other work through their feelings, creating a safe environment for vulnerability and growth. It also reminds couples to invite God into their emotional challenges, trusting Him to provide the strength and guidance to overcome fear and frustration.

If your husband struggles to share his emotions or seems closed off, it doesn't mean he doesn't care. Many men face pressures that make vulnerability difficult. Through your prayers, patience, and understanding, you can create a space where he feels safe to open up, trusting that God is healing and softening his heart in ways you may not see.

Ultimately, this verse challenges us to reject a spirit of fear or negativity and instead embrace the power, love, and self-control that God provides through His Spirit. By leaning on these divine gifts, couples can strengthen their emotional connection, resolve conflicts with grace, and experience the peace that comes from walking in step with God. Relying on God's Spirit together transforms struggles into a path toward more profound understanding and unity, demonstrating how emotions can be a place of growth when surrendered to Him.

REFLECTION:

1. How do I respond when my husband is stressed or emotional?

Do my responses to his emotions reflect patience and understanding, or do they add to his stress? How can I create a calming and supportive atmosphere when he's overwhelmed?

2. Are there ways I could be more patient or understanding when he's struggling?

What specific situations reveal my tendencies to be impatient or dismissive? How can I ask God to shape my heart to respond with empathy and grace?

3. How can I create an environment where he feels safe sharing his emotions with me?

Am I actively listening and validating his feelings, or do I unintentionally shut him down? What practical steps can I take to make him feel heard and valued?

PRAYER:

"Lord, you know my husband's challenges, and I lift up his emotions to you. Bring him peace and give him strength to handle stress. Help him to rest in your promises, knowing you are with him always. Let him find calm in your presence. Amen."

TODAY'S CALL TO ACTION:

Observe your husband's emotional state today. Offer a listening ear without judgment and let him know you are there to support him. Commit to praying for peace in his heart.

Day 5

CHARACTER

"But the fruit of the Spirit is love, joy, peace..."

Megan always admired her husband, Ryan, for his determination and drive. He was the kind of man who worked hard to provide for their family, rarely complained, and was always willing to help a friend in need. However, one area that Megan quietly prayed about was Ryan's temper. While he was never cruel or unkind, Ryan had a short fuse when things didn't go as planned. Whether it was a frustrating delay at work, a driver cutting him off in traffic, or even a minor mishap at home, Megan often saw his frustration bubble over into anger. She worried about how this might impact their two young boys, who were starting to notice and even mimic their dad's reactions.

One particular Saturday morning, Ryan decided to tackle a backyard project—building a treehouse for their boys.

Megan smiled as she watched him gather tools and sketch a plan, excited to see how this fun project would unfold. The boys followed him around the yard like ducklings, chattering about their future "fort," and Megan could see how much Ryan loved spending time with them.

But by mid-afternoon, things started to go sideways. Ryan struggled with the measurements, and a wrong cut on a large piece of wood set him back an hour. Then, a drill bit broke, and one of the boys accidentally knocked over a can of paint, spilling it all over the freshly cut planks. Ryan's face turned red, and Megan braced herself for the explosion she had seen so many times before.

Sure enough, Ryan shouted in frustration, startling the boys. "I can't deal with this right now!" he barked, throwing his gloves down and storming off to the garage. The boys stood frozen, their excitement replaced with confusion and fear. Megan knelt down, comforting them as she fought back tears. She loved Ryan deeply but hated seeing these moments where his frustration overtook him.

Later that evening, after the boys were in bed, Megan decided to have a heart-to-heart with Ryan. She approached him gently, sitting down beside him on the couch. "Hey," she began softly. "I know today didn't go as planned and I know that you wanted everything to go perfectly for the boys. But I think they were more excited to spend time with you than have a perfect treehouse."

Ryan sighed, his shoulders slumping. "I blew it, didn't I?" he said quietly. "I saw the look on their faces, and I hated it. I don't want them to remember me as the dad who loses his temper over small stuff."

Megan reached for his hand. "It's not too late to change that," she said. "You're an amazing dad, Ryan. I see how much you love them, and they see it too. But maybe this is something we can pray about together. God can help you with this. It's not something you have to fix on your own."

Ryan nodded, humbled by her words. That night, Megan prayed with him, asking God to give him patience and self-control, especially in moments of frustration. Ryan admitted to God, and to himself, that he didn't want to let anger dictate his reactions anymore.

Over the next few weeks, Megan noticed small but significant changes in Ryan. When things went wrong, he paused, took a deep breath, and asked for a moment to gather himself before responding. The boys, seeing their dad approach problems with calm instead of anger, started to reflect that same attitude. One evening, as they worked together to finish the treehouse, Ryan laughed off a mistake, joking with the boys that "every fort needs a little character." Megan's heart swelled as she watched her husband model grace and resilience for their children.

For Megan, this journey reminded her that real character growth happens over time and with God's help. It also deepened her respect for Ryan, seeing his willingness to acknowledge his struggles and seek God's guidance. For Ryan, it was a lesson in humility and reliance on God's strength. And for their boys, it was a glimpse of what it means to face life's frustrations with patience, love, and trust in the Lord.

"But the fruit of the Spirit is love, joy, peace, forbear-
ance, kindness, goodness, faithfulness, gentleness
and self-control. Against such things there is no
law."– Galatians 5:22-23 (NIV)

This passage highlights the qualities that the Holy Spirit produces in a believer's life. These fruits are evidence of a heart transformed by God, reflecting His character and enabling us to live in a way that pleases Him and blesses others. Unlike fleeting emotions or outward behaviors, these traits are deep-rooted and enduring, shaping how we interact with our families, communities, and the world.

In the story, Ryan's struggle with patience and gentleness in his parenting illustrates the challenges of growing in godly character. His frustration with his children and his initial responses reveal the tension between human tendencies and the Spirit's work in us. This verse reminds us that the fruit of the Spirit is not something we can produce on our own—it is the result of walking closely with God and allowing His Spirit to refine us daily.

For Ryan, the realizing that he needs God's help to be more patient and gentle with his children is a turning point. As he surrenders his parenting to the Spirit's guidance, he begins to see these fruits develop in his life, fostering a healthier, more loving relationship with his kids. His growth demonstrates how allowing the Spirit to work within us transforms our character and positively influences those around us.

The application of this verse challenges believers to examine their lives and ask whether the fruit of the Spirit is evident in their thoughts, words, and actions. Are we responding to situations with love, patience,

> Unlike fleeting emotions or outward behaviors, these traits are deep-rooted and enduring, shaping how we interact with our families, communities, and the world.

and kindness? Do we reflect gentleness and self-control in moments of stress or conflict? This passage calls us to daily dependence on the Holy Spirit, recognizing that true character transformation comes from Him, not our efforts alone.

In the context of family and marriage, this verse is particularly powerful. It reminds us that godly character is essential for building strong, loving relationships. For Ryan, embodying the fruit of the Spirit in his parenting allows him to nurture his children's hearts and point them to Christ. For all believers, this passage invites us to seek God's Spirit continually, trusting Him to cultivate a character that glorifies Him and blesses those we love.

By walking in the Spirit, we reflect God's love and faithfulness in all areas of life, becoming living testimonies of His transformative power. For Ryan, this growth not only shapes his relationship with his children but also strengthens his own faith, reminding him that God is always at work, even in the small, everyday moments.

Your husband's spiritual journey may not look like yours, and that's okay. God works uniquely in each of our lives, shaping us in His time and in His way. Whether your husband is eager to grow or uncertain about his faith, your prayers are powerful. Trust that God hears you and is moving, even when the progress seems slow or invisible.

REFLECTION:

1. What qualities in my husband's character do I admire and appreciate?

Have I taken time to reflect on and affirm the specific traits in my husband that reflect Christ-like character? How can I express my gratitude for these qualities in a way that encourages him?

2. Are there areas in my own character that I need to grow in to support him better?

What personal habits or attitudes might hinder me from fully supporting my husband's growth? How can I ask God to transform these areas and align my heart with His design for our marriage?

3. How can I pray on his behalf for specific character traits, like patience or kindness?

What challenges or pressures might be shaping my husband's character right now? How can I intentionally pray for God to strengthen and refine his heart in these areas?

PRAYER:

"God, I pray for my husband's character to grow in the image of Christ. Help him to cultivate patience, kindness, and humility. Strengthen his faith, and let your Spirit produce fruit in his life that blesses everyone around him, especially our family. Amen."

TODAY'S CALL TO ACTION:

Identify one character trait in your husband that you admire and tell him how it inspires you. Pray over a particular area where you hope to see continued growth.

Day 6

PARENTING

"Fathers, do not provoke your children to anger..."

E mily and Chris were parents to two energetic boys, Liam and Noah, ages six and eight. Chris was a loving and dedicated father who worked hard to provide for his family. Still, his approach to parenting was heavily influenced by how he was raised.

Growing up, his dad was strict and no-nonsense, believing discipline was the key to raising respectful children. Chris adopted this mindset, often stepping in to correct the boys firmly when they acted out. On the other hand, Emily leaned toward a gentler approach, trying to explain the consequences and encourage the boys with positive reinforcement. The difference in their parenting styles often caused tension between them.

One Saturday afternoon, the family decided to go to the

park for a picnic. While Emily set up their lunch, the boys began chasing each other with sticks, laughing and yelling. Worried they might hurt themselves or someone else, Chris shouted across the park, "Liam! Noah! Knock it off!" His voice was loud and sharp, and both boys froze, dropping the sticks immediately. But instead of looking remorseful, they looked scared.

As they returned to the picnic blanket, Emily noticed Liam's eyes welling up with tears. He sat down quietly, picking at his sandwich without eating, and Noah avoided eye contact with his dad. The mood had shifted, and Emily's heart broke as she watched her typically playful boys retreat into themselves. She glanced at Chris, who seemed frustrated and oblivious to the impact of his words.

That night, after the boys were asleep, Emily brought it up. She prayed first, asking God to help her approach Chris with love, not criticism. Sitting beside him on the couch, she started gently. "Chris, I know you're trying to keep the boys safe and teach them to listen, and I love that you care so much about them. But I think sometimes they respond to your tone more than your words. When you yelled at them today, they looked scared, not like they understood what they did wrong."

Chris frowned, clearly uncomfortable. "I'm just trying to make sure they don't get hurt," he said defensively. "If I don't stop them right away, who knows what could happen?"

Emily nodded. "I get that. But what if we could handle it in a way that teaches them to think about their actions without making them afraid of you? They look up to you so much, Chris. I know they'll learn more if they feel like you're on their side."

Chris was quiet for a long moment. Finally, he sighed. "I don't want to be the dad who always yells. I guess I just don't know how else to handle it."

Emily placed a hand on his. "We're a team, and we can figure it out together. Maybe we can pray about this and ask God to help us parent in a way that shows both love and guidance. And I'll do my part to back you up when the boys need correction—I don't want you to feel like it's all on you."

Chris nodded, his shoulders relaxing. "Thanks for saying that. I know I can be hard on them, but I want them to grow up knowing I love them. And I don't want them to grow up scared to come to me if they are ever in trouble and need help."

Over the next few weeks, Chris consciously worked to change his approach. When the boys misbehaved, he paused before reacting, taking a breath and lowering his voice. Chris started explaining why their actions weren't okay instead of simply demanding they stop. He also made a point to praise them when they did something right, like sharing toys or helping clean up, which Emily noticed made a big difference in their behavior.

One evening, as the family sat down for dinner, Noah accidentally knocked over a glass of milk. Instead of reacting with frustration, Chris calmly handed him a paper towel and said, "It's okay, buddy. Let's clean it up together." Noah's eyes lit up with relief, and he smiled as he helped his dad. Emily's heart swelled as she watched Chris model patience and kindness.

Chris also began spending more intentional time with the boys, whether tossing a football in the backyard or helping them with their homework. The boys started opening up to him more, sharing their thoughts and feelings in a way they hadn't before. Emily watched as their relationship with Chris grew, and that brought her so much joy.

For Chris, this journey was humbling but rewarding. He realized that parenting wasn't just about enforcing rules but building trust, teaching through love, and showing his sons how to handle life's challenges with grace. It was a reminder for Emily that prayer and gentle encouragement could lead to real change in her husband and their family dynamic. Together, they were learning to be the parents God had called them to be—parents who guided their children with a balance of love, discipline, and faith.

"Fathers, do not exasperate your children; instead, bring them up in the training and instruction of the Lord." –Ephesians 6:4 (NIV)

This verse is a foundational directive for parenting, particularly for fathers. It emphasizes both responsibility and approach to raising children. It calls for a balance of discipline and nurture, warning against actions that provoke frustration or discouragement in children. Instead, it encourages parents to focus on spiritual guidance and godly instruction, reflecting Christ's grace, patience, and love.

In the story, Chris's struggle to balance discipline with understanding illustrates a common challenge for parents. His frustration leads to interactions that exasperate his children, creating tension rather than teaching.This verse reminds men that their role as fathers is not merely correcting behavior but shepherding their children's hearts toward God. As Chris learns to pair discipline with encouragement, he models a patient love that reflects God's fatherly care.

The application of this verse challenges parents to evaluate how their actions and attitudes influence their children's emotional and spiritual growth. Are their words and actions

> Parents are called to guide their children with wisdom, setting boundaries while also providing encouragement and support.

building their children up or tearing them down? Discipline is essential, but this verse warns against harshness or unfair expectations that can damage a child's confidence or trust. Instead, parents are called to guide their children with wisdom, setting boundaries while also providing encouragement and support.

The verse also highlights the importance of prioritizing spiritual instruction. Raising children up "in the training and instruction of the Lord" involves more than attending church or saying prayers at mealtime—it's about creating a home environment where faith is lived out daily. For Chris, this means modeling humility, seeking God's wisdom in parenting decisions, and sharing biblical truths with his children in a way that resonates with their unique personalities.

Ultimately, this verse reminds parents that their role is not to control their children but to nurture them in a way that reflects God's love and prepares them for a lifelong relationship with Him. For Chris, embracing this approach transforms his parenting from a source of stress to an opportunity to build trust, strengthen his bond with his kids, and point them to Christ. For all parents, this verse guides us to raise children with grace, wisdom, and the ultimate goal of leading them closer to the Lord.

REFLECTION:

1. How do we work together in parenting our children, and how can I support him in this role?

Are there specific parenting decisions or dynamics where I could better affirm his contributions? How can I encourage him in a way that strengthens our partnership and honors his role as a father?

2. What can I do to make him feel respected and valued as a father?

Do my words and actions consistently communicate respect for his parenting style, even when it differs from mine? How can I intentionally highlight his strengths as a father?

3. Are there areas of parenting we need to pray about together for wisdom and guidance?

What parenting challenges or opportunities might we benefit from lifting up in prayer? How can we create a habit of praying together for our children and their future?

PRAYER:

"Heavenly Father, thank you for my husband's role as a father. Give him wisdom to parent with love and consistency. Help him to model Christ's love for our children and to raise them with strength and compassion. Let his heart be patient and full of grace. Amen."

TODAY'S CALL TO ACTION:

Acknowledge your husband's unique contributions as a father by affirming something he does well with your children. Pray together about an area where you both desire God's wisdom in parenting.

Day 7

AS HUSBAND

"...demonstrate love for your wives with the same tender devotion..."

C laire had always been drawn to Tom's steady, reliable nature. From the moment they met, she knew he was the kind of man she could count on—a man of his word who showed his love through actions rather than flowery words or grand gestures. In their early years of marriage, this grounded her, giving her a sense of security and stability. But over time, Claire found herself wishing for more overt expressions of love. She missed the spontaneous romance she saw in other couples, the thoughtful surprises, or the gushing "I love yous" that her friends often posted on social media.

One evening, after a long day, Claire sat at the dining table scrolling through her phone while Tom worked on fixing a leaky faucet in the bathroom. She came across a post from a friend whose husband had surprised her with flowers and a handwritten letter for no special reason. Claire sighed and put down her phone, feeling a pang of disappointment. Tom hadn't bought her flowers in years, and while he was always kind and respectful, she sometimes felt like they had settled into a routine that lacked the spark she longed for.

Later that night, after Tom had finished fixing the faucet and gone to bed, Claire stayed up journaling. She poured out her feelings, writing about her desire to feel more loved and cherished. But as she reflected, she felt a nudge in her heart. It was a gentle reminder of how Tom had shown his love, even if he didn't wrap them in romance.

She remembered how he always filled her car with gas without her ever asking, how he never missed a chance to ask if she needed anything when he ran errands and how he rubbed her shoulders after a long day without expecting anything in return. These weren't flashy or dramatic gestures but they were steady, dependable acts of love.

The following day, Claire decided to look for ways to appreciate the love Tom already showed. As she poured her coffee, she noticed a sticky note on the machine that read, "Don't forget to smile today. You're amazing!" It was Tom's handwriting, and she felt a rush of gratitude. She glanced at the calendar and realized it was the anniversary of the day they'd met—a day he always quietly remembered. For the first time in a while, she felt a deep sense of gratitude for his thoughtfulness.

That evening, after dinner, Claire sat down beside Tom on

the couch. "Hey," she started, leaning into him. "I just wanted to say thank you. I know I don't always notice it in the moment, but you show me love in so many ways. I see it in how you care for me, and I want you to know it means a lot."

Tom looked at her, surprised. "You don't have to thank me for that," he said with a small smile. "I just want to make sure you're taken care of. It's what I'm here for."

That conversation shifted something for Claire. She started paying more attention to Tom's quiet acts of love—the way he always checked her tires before a road trip, how he remembered to make her favorite tea when she wasn't feeling well, and how he kissed her goodnight every single evening. The more she noticed, the more her heart softened, and the less she felt the need for grand gestures. She realized that love wasn't about comparison or meeting a certain standard—it was about recognizing the unique ways her husband cared for her.

Over time, Claire found ways to express her gratitude more openly. She started leaving little notes of encouragement for Tom or thanking him for specific things he did, like mowing the lawn or fixing things around the house. One Saturday morning, as they worked in the garden, she looked over at him and said, "You're my favorite part of this life." Tom paused, then smiled shyly. "You're mine, too," he said, and that moment filled Claire with a joy she couldn't explain.

Claire realized that her prayers for a deeper connection with her husband had been answered, not by changing Tom but by changing her perspective. She had learned to see and celebrate his love in all the small, steady ways it showed up, and in doing so, she fell in love with him all over again. Tom, too, felt encouraged by her new appreciation and started finding small ways to express his love in ways that felt natural to him. Together, they rediscovered the beauty of their partnership—a quiet, steady love built on mutual care, respect, and gratitude.

"And to the husbands, you are to demonstrate love for your wives with the same tender devotion that Christ demonstrated to us, his bride. For he died for us..." –Ephesians 5:25 (TPT)

> **Christ's love is selfless, enduring, and centered on the well-being of others.**

This verse sets a high standard for husbands, calling them to love their wives with the same sacrificial, unconditional love Christ has for the church. Christ's love is selfless, enduring, and centered on the well-being of others. This concept challenges husbands to prioritize their wives' needs above their own and create a marriage reflecting Christ's humility, care, and commitment.

In the story, Tom's quiet but consistent ways of showing love mirror this biblical principle. While his expressions of love may not be flashy or dramatic, they demonstrate a deep, sacrificial care for his wife, Claire. His actions, like fixing things around the house and creating a stable environment for their family, align with the self-giving love described in this verse. However, it also challenges Claire to recognize and value his Christ-like love, even when it doesn't always align with her expectations.

This verse's application is transformative for both husbands and wives. For husbands, it calls for a love that is not based on feelings or circumstances but on a commitment to serve and cherish their wives in all seasons. This means being patient, forgiving, and intentionally showing love, even in times of conflict or difficulty. It also encourages husbands to consider their wives' spiritual, emotional, and physical needs, ensuring their leadership is rooted in humility and care.

This verse provides a perspective for wives that can help them appreciate their husbands' love, even when it's expressed differently than they might expect. Claire realizes that Tom's steady actions reflect sacrificial love and that it is vital to recognize and affirm how her husband fulfills this calling.

Every marriage looks different, and some husbands may struggle to express love in easily recognized ways. Whether your husband is naturally affectionate or reserved, your encouragement and prayers can nurture the bond between you, trusting that God sees and works through every effort.

Ultimately, this verse reminds couples that marriage is designed to reflect Christ's relationship with the church—a love marked by sacrifice, grace, and unwavering commitment. When husbands love their wives in this way, they create a safe and nurturing environment where trust and intimacy can thrive. For Tom and Claire, embracing this biblical model of love strengthens their bond, helping them grow closer to each other and God. For all couples, this verse serves as both a guide and a challenge to make their marriage a living testimony of Christ's love.

REFLECTION:

1. What are some simple ways I can make my husband feel loved and cherished?

Am I attentive to how my husband feels most loved, such as through words, actions, or quality time? How can I intentionally express love in a way that speaks to his heart?

2. Do I focus more on what he does wrong or what he does right?

How often do I express gratitude or praise for the things he does well? How can I shift my mindset and communication to celebrate his strengths rather than magnify his weaknesses?

3. How can I show love to him that makes him feel special and appreciated?

What specific gestures or habits could I incorporate into our daily lives to remind him that he is deeply valued? How can I ask God to give me creativity and thoughtfulness to nurture our connection?

PRAYER:

"Lord, I am so grateful for my husband. Help him to feel loved, valued, and cherished. Teach him to love me in the same way you love your church. I pray for deep connection between us so that our marriage will glorify you and inspire others. Amen."

TODAY'S CALL TO ACTION:

Do one small act of love today—like a hug, a compliment, or making his favorite meal—to show your husband he is cherished. Reflect on how God calls you to love him intentionally.

Day 8

COMMUNITY

"And let us consider how we may spur one another on towards love and good deeds..."

Michael and Heather had recently moved to a new town for Michael's job, leaving behind the familiar rhythms of their old neighborhood, church, and friends. At first, they were excited about the change—a fresh start in a beautiful area with new opportunities. However, as the months passed, Heather began to notice subtle changes in Michael. Once upbeat and optimistic, he now seemed withdrawn and preoccupied. He spent his evenings scrolling on his phone or watching TV, but he rarely smiled or laughed like he used to.

Heather knew the transition had been harder for Michael than he had let on. He had been part of a men's Bible study group in their old town that met every Thursday morning. It had been his anchor, where Michael could share his struggles and hear wisdom from men he trusted. He had also served as an usher at their church, which he genuinely enjoyed. Now, he seemed adrift with no close friends and no ministry to connect with.

One evening, as they cleaned up after dinner, Heather gently broached the subject. "I've been thinking," she began. "We haven't really found our people here yet. I know it's been a big adjustment for both of us, but I wonder if it's time to start looking for a church or a small group."

Michael shrugged, not meeting her eyes. "I know we need to," he said, "but I'm just tired. It feels like starting over, and I don't know if I have the energy for that right now."

Heather nodded, understanding his reluctance. Moving was exhausting, and putting yourself out there to build new relationships could be daunting. But she also knew how much community had meant to Michael in the past. She decided to pray about it. That night, she prayed for God to stir Michael's heart and motivate him to seek connection again.

A few weeks later, Heather stumbled across a flyer at the local coffee shop for a nearby church hosting a men's breakfast. She casually mentioned it to Michael, who hesitated but eventually agreed to check it out. "It's just breakfast, right?" he said. "What's the harm in going?"

That Saturday morning, Michael returned from the breakfast looking lighter than Heather had seen him in months. "How was it?" she asked as he set his keys on the counter. Michael smiled, a rare sight lately. "It was actually...good," he said. "The guys were welcoming; some invited me to a weekly Bible study. I think I might go next week."

Over the following weeks, Michael began attending the study regularly. It didn't take long for him to form connections with a few of the men. They shared openly about their challenges—balancing work and family, maintaining faith in a busy world, and dealing with personal struggles. Michael realized how much he had missed having a space where he could be honest and hear encouragement from others walking a similar path.

The impact on Michael's emotional and spiritual health was profound. He came home after each meeting with a renewed sense of purpose and joy. Heather noticed he started praying more intentionally and initiating spiritual conversations with her—something he hadn't done in months. He even suggested they attend the church together, which became another step in rebuilding their sense of belonging.

One evening, as they sat together on the porch, Michael turned to Heather and said, "I didn't realize how much I needed this. I was trying to handle everything on my own, but having people walk alongside me made such a difference. I really think God used you to push me in the right direction."

Heather smiled, her heart full. She realized that community wasn't just about having friends to hang out with—it was about spiritual growth, emotional support, and accountability that helps you stay anchored in your faith. For Michael, the men in his small group became a lifeline, reminding him that he wasn't alone and that God's design for the church included the gift of fellowship.

As they continued to build relationships in their new town, Michael and Heather grew closer as a couple. They began hosting small gatherings at their home, opening their doors to new friends and neighbors. They learned that building community wasn't always easy, but it was deeply rewarding, and essential for their spiritual and emotional wellbeing.

"And let us consider how we may spur one another on towards love and good deeds, not giving up meeting together, as some are in the habit of doing, but encouraging one another-- and all the more as you see the Day approaching." – Hebrews 10:24-25 (NIV)

Hebrews emphasizes the essential role of community in the Christian life. God never intended for us to walk our faith journey alone; instead, He calls us to be part of a supportive and encouraging fellowship. Being in community with other believers provides accountability, shared wisdom, and the spiritual strength to persevere in love and good works.

Michael's isolation and weariness reflect the challenges of trying to navigate life without strong connections to a faith-based community. His return to church and involvement in a men's group encouraged him. It brought him spiritual renewal, showing how community can revive both emotional and spiritual wellbeing.

The verse's reminder to "not neglect meeting together" directly applies to Michael's experience. His choice to recon-nect with others in faith is trans-formative, reminding him of the

> Being in community with other believers provides accountability, shared wisdom, and the spiritual strength to persevere in love and good works.

joy and strength found in walking alongside other believers. It illustrates how community helps us focus outwardly, stirring one another toward love and good works rather than being consumed by personal struggles.

The application extends to all believers: Engaging in meaningful relationships within a faith community equips us to live out our calling, face challenges with support, and grow deeper in our walk with Christ. For Michael, it's not just about finding friends. It's about reigniting his sense of purpose and aligning his life with God's plan through the encouragement of others.

REFLECTION:

1. How can we, as a couple, serve our community or church together?

Can we use shared passions or strengths to bless others in our community? How can we prayerfully discern opportunities to serve together as a reflection of Christ's love?

2. How can I encourage my husband to engage in meaningful connections that build both him and our community?

What strengths or interests does he have that could naturally lend themselves to serving or connecting with others? Am I willing to step out alongside him to foster relationships that strengthen our marriage and community?

3. How can I pray for him to be a positive influence in our community?

What specific qualities or opportunities can I lift up in prayer, asking God to use him to impact others for His glory? How can I encourage him to step confidently into his God-given role as a light in our community?

PRAYER:

"God, thank You for the gift of community and the way You've designed us to live connected—not just to You, but to one another. I lift up my husband today and ask that You would gently stir his heart toward meaningful connection.

When he feels isolated or overwhelmed, remind him that he doesn't have to carry everything alone. Surround him with godly men who will walk beside him, encourage him, challenge him, and speak truth into his life.

Restore any places in his heart that have grown weary or withdrawn. Heal the silent discouragement that often comes with disconnection. Help him to know that needing others is not weakness—it's part of Your design. Give him the courage to take a step toward community, even when it feels uncomfortable or unfamiliar. And show me how to support and encourage him in that journey.

Build up his emotional and spiritual health through authentic relationships. May his soul be refreshed as he finds people who truly see him, listen well, and point him back to You. And in turn, may he become that kind of friend to others. Let our home be a place where community grows and where Your presence is felt in every conversation, meal, and moment we share with others. Amen."

TODAY'S CALL TO ACTION:

Take five minutes to brainstorm a list of 3–5 people (or couples) you and your husband could reach out to this month. Think about those who might also be looking for deeper connection—whether it's a neighbor, a coworker, someone from church, or an old friend you've lost touch

with. Choose one name together and make a simple plan—
invite them over for coffee, a game night, or a casual dinner.
Don't overthink it. The goal isn't to entertain—it's to connect.
Pray over that list together and ask God to begin something
meaningful through it.

Day 9

SERVICE

"The Son of Man came not to be served but to serve..."

C arla had always admired her husband, Tim, for his servant's heart. Whether helping a neighbor fix a broken fence, volunteering at the local food pantry, or organizing church fundraisers, Tim approached service with enthusiasm and humility.

For him, serving others wasn't an obligation. It was an extension of his faith and a way to reflect God's love. Watching him in action often reminded Carla of Jesus washing His disciples' feet, a quiet act of love that spoke volumes.

One Saturday morning, Carla stood at the window, sipping her coffee and watching Tim load tools into the back of his truck. He had volunteered to help a single mom from their church repair her leaky roof before the next storm rolled in. "Do you want me to come with you?" Carla asked, stepping onto the porch.

Tim smiled. "I've got it," he said, kissing her on the cheek. "But maybe you could bake something to bring over later. I'm sure the kids would love some cookies."

Carla nodded, struck once again by how naturally service flowed from him. She decided to tag along later with the baked goods and was moved to see Tim not only repairing the roof but also taking time to teach the young boys how to hammer nails safely. By the end of the day, the roof was fixed, and the family had gained a sense of security and gratitude that shone through their smiles.

That evening, as Carla and Tim sat together on the couch, she brought up something that had been on her heart. "You're always so willing to serve," she said, leaning into him. "It's one of the things I love most about you. But have you ever considered why it's so important to you?"

Tim thought for a moment. "I guess I've always felt that everything we have—our time, skills, and resources—comes from God," he said. "It doesn't feel right to hold onto it all when I see others in need. I think about how Jesus didn't just preach to people—He fed them, healed them, and met their needs. If I can do even a fraction of that, I feel like I'm honoring Him."

Carla nodded, feeling her heart swell with admiration.

"It's inspiring," she said. "You remind me that serving isn't just about fixing things; it's about showing people they're seen and loved."

A few weeks later, their church organized a community outreach event to clean up a local park and build a playground for kids in a low-income neighborhood. Tim eagerly signed up and invited Carla and their teenage daughter, Lily, to join him. At first, Lily grumbled, reluctant to give up her Saturday. But as the day progressed, Carla watched her daughter's attitude change. She saw Lily laughing as she painted benches and cheering with the neighborhood kids as they tested the new swings. By the end of the day, Lily was already asking when the next event would be.

That night, Carla reflected on how Tim's consistent example of service had influenced their entire family. She realized that his heart for giving back had blessed those around them and planted seeds of compassion and generosity in their own home. She made a mental note to thank God for a husband who led by example, quietly showing his family how to live out their faith.

For Carla, this was a reminder that a life of service isn't about grand gestures or recognition. It's about being willing to step into the needs around you with humility and love. Watching Tim joyfully serve others inspired her to look for new ways to give back and appreciate their unique role in reflecting God's love to the world.

"For even the Son of Man did not come to be served, but to serve, and to give his life as a ransom for many." – Mark 10:45 (NIV)

Mark highlights Christ's ultimate example of servant leadership. Jesus, the Son of God, chose not to demand honor or privileges but to humble Himself and serve others sacrificially. His life teaches us that true greatness is found not in being served but in serving others out of love and obedience to God. Service is central to living a Christ-like life, transforming not only those we help but also our hearts.

> All acts of service are valuable when done with a heart of love and obedience to God.

Tim reflects this principle by serving his community with humility and joy. His actions remind us that service is not just about meeting practical needs. It's about showing others the love of Christ through our willingness to give of ourselves. Tim's example inspires his family, showing how a servant's heart can leave a legacy of compassion and faith for others to follow. But Tim didn't always serve on his own. He often included his family, finding ways for them to participate in acts of service, no matter how small. Whether bringing cookies to volunteers or helping with a clean-up day, shared experiences become opportunities for families to grow closer, create lasting memories, and teach children the joy of giving.

This shared service illustrates an important truth: the

significance of an act isn't determined by its size. Whether organizing a significant outreach event or contributing something small, all acts of service are valuable when done with a heart of love and obedience to God. For Tim, serving alone or with his family wasn't about measuring significance. It was about answering God's call to love and serve in whatever way they could. This mindset encouraged his family to embrace service as a way of life, reminding them that every act of kindness can have a profound impact, no matter how small.

The verse also challenges us to examine our motivations for service. Just as Christ gave Himself selflessly, we are called to serve without seeking recognition or personal gain. Tim's genuine care for others mirrors this attitude, reminding us that when we serve with Christ-like humility, we reflect God's heart to the world.

The application for all believers is clear: embracing a life of service honors God *and* deepens our faith and relationships. Like Tim, we can find joy and purpose in serving others, knowing that our efforts—no matter how small—are part of God's more excellent plan to show His love and redemption to the world. Serving together as a family or individually allows us to participate in God's work and experience the transformative power of giving.

REFLECTION:

1. What are some ways I've noticed my husband serving others?

Do I take time to acknowledge and celebrate how my husband serves, big and small? How can I affirm his heart for service and encourage him to continue reflecting Christ's example?

2. Do I encourage his heart to serve, or do I sometimes focus on my own needs?

Am I balancing my personal expectations with a genuine appreciation for his service? How can I pray for a selfless heart that supports his calling to serve others?

3. How can I be a better partner and serve others alongside him?

What shared service opportunities could strengthen our bond and our witness to others? How can I pray for wisdom and unity as we serve together as a couple?

PRAYER:

"Lord Jesus, you were a servant leader. I pray my husband would follow in your steps, serving others joyfully. Help him to see the needs around him and to respond in love. Let him find fulfillment and purpose in service. Amen."

TODAY'S CALL TO ACTION:

Encourage your husband in one area where he serves others, whether at home, work, or in the community. Let him know you see and appreciate his heart for service.

Day 10

JOB / PROFESSION

"Whatever you do, work heartily, as for the Lord."

Amanda had always admired her husband, Jake, for his strong work ethic. From the moment they met, he had been a man of integrity who gave his best to everything he did. Lately, however, Amanda has noticed a change. Jake came home from work each evening looking tired and discouraged, his once-passionate conversations about his job now replaced with silence or short responses. Amanda knew he wasn't happy anymore, but Jake hadn't said much about it, and she didn't want to push him.

One evening, as they sat together after dinner, Amanda decided to gently bring it up. "Jake, I've noticed you've been pretty quiet about work lately. Is everything okay?" she asked, placing her hand on his.

Jake sighed and leaned back in his chair. "It's just... I feel like I'm spinning my wheels," he admitted. "I do the same thing every day, and it feels meaningless. I'm not sure this is what I want to do anymore, but I don't know what else is out there. We've got bills to pay, and I can't just walk away from a steady paycheck."

Amanda's heart ached for him. She could see how much the lack of fulfillment weighed on him, but she also knew Jake's heart. He wanted his work to matter, not just to earn a living but to feel like he was contributing to something meaningful. "Have you prayed about it?" she asked softly.

Jake hesitated, then shook his head. "Not really. I guess I've been trying to figure it out on my alone."

Amanda gently squeezed his hand. "Maybe we can pray about it together. I believe God has a plan for you, Jake—something that will provide for our family and give you a sense of purpose."

That night, they sat together on the couch, and Amanda led them in a simple prayer. She asked God to give Jake clarity and wisdom, bless his hands' work, and open doors if a new opportunity was His will. Jake seemed hesitant at first, but as Amanda prayed, she felt him relax, his grip on her hand tightening as if he were letting go of some of the weight he had been carrying.

Over the next few weeks, Amanda continued to pray for Jake daily. She asked God not only to bless his work but to help him work with excellence, even in a role that no longer inspired him. She asked God to bless his work and help him work with excellence, even in a role that no longer inspired him.. She also prayed for his heart to be open to whatever God had in store, whether it was a new opportunity or a renewed sense of purpose where he was.

One evening, Jake came home with a different energy. "You'll never guess what happened today," he said, setting down his bag. "I was talking to a coworker who mentioned a position opening in another department. It's something I've always been interested in, and I think I will apply."

Amanda's face lit up. "That's amazing, Jake! I'm so proud of you."

Jake applied for the position, and as the weeks passed, Amanda noticed a shift in him. He was putting extra effort into his current role, determined to leave a positive impression no matter what happened with the new opportunity. It reminded Amanda of the verse from Colossians: "Whatever you do, work at it with all your heart, as working for the Lord, not for human masters." She realized that Jake was beginning to see his work as a job and a way to honor God.

When the new position was offered to him, Jake was overjoyed. It was a role that allowed him to use his gifts in ways he hadn't been able to before, and Amanda could see the spark of purpose returning to his eyes. That evening, as they celebrated, Jake said, "I know I wouldn't have had the courage to go for this if you hadn't encouraged me to pray and trust God. Thank you for believing in me."

For Amanda, it was a reminder of the power of prayer—not just to change circumstances but to shift hearts in the process. She continued to pray for Jake, asking God to bless the work of his hands and to give him fulfillment and joy in his profession. Watching him thrive in his new role was a gift that reminded her of God's faithfulness and His desire to bless the work we do when we entrust it to Him.

"Whatever you do, work at it with all your heart, as working for the Lord, not for human masters." – Colossians 3:23 (NIV)

This verse reminds believers that all work, whether mundane or challenging, is an opportunity to honor God. Approaching our jobs with the mindset that we are ultimately working for the Lord transforms our perspective. Work becomes more than just a way to earn a living—it becomes a form of worship, a place to demonstrate integrity, diligence, and faithfulness.

Jake's struggle to find fulfillment in his career reflects a common challenge. When he shifts his focus to working "as for the Lord," it renews his motivation and brings a sense of purpose to his profession. The verse encourages believers like Jake to view their work as part of God's mission, where even small tasks can glorify Him when done with excellence and a faithful heart.

> Approaching our jobs with the mindset that we are ultimately working for the Lord transforms our perspective.

The application of this verse challenges us to give our best in every role, knowing that our efforts matter to God. It also reminds us to trust God with our careers, recognizing that He has a plan for our work and will bless it when we commit it to Him. Jake's journey shows how this mindset transforms our approach to work and impacts those around us, as a godly work ethic and attitude can serve as a powerful testimony to coworkers and others.

By seeing our work as a service to the Lord, we can find joy and purpose, even in seasons of uncertainty or struggle, trusting that God is using our efforts for His glory and our growth.

REFLECTION:

1. How can I support my husband in his job or career, especially during stressful seasons?

Am I intentional about offering encouragement when he faces challenges at work? How can I create a safe space where he feels valued and supported, regardless of professional pressures?

2. Do I take the time to listen when he shares about his work?

Am I truly present and engaged when he discusses his work, or do I get distracted by my own concerns? How can I show interest in his career and make him feel that his efforts matter?

3. What specific challenges in his work can I pray about to help him feel uplifted?

Are there particular struggles or uncertainties in his job that I can bring to God in prayer? How can I intercede for his professional growth, integrity, and fulfillment?

PRAYER:

"Father, thank you for my husband's work. I pray he will approach his job with integrity and excellence, honoring you in everything he does. Let him testify to your goodness in his workplace as he brings peace and diligence to his work environment. Amen."

TODAY'S CALL TO ACTION:

Ask your husband about his day at work and listen attentively. Offer a specific prayer for him regarding a challenge or opportunity he's navigating in his job.

Day 11

HEALTH

"Your body is a temple of the Holy Spirit.."

Rachel had always admired her husband Sam's determination and dedication, but lately, she'd started to worry about him. Sam worked long hours as a manager at a busy logistics company, often skipping meals or grabbing fast food on the go. He spent evenings on the couch at home, too tired to do much more than watch TV. Exercise had entirely fallen off his radar, and his once-active lifestyle now seemed like a distant memory. Rachel noticed he was putting on weight, often seemed short of breath, and wasn't sleeping well. She was concerned but didn't want to come across as critical or nagging.

Rachel brought it up one evening gently after the kids were in bed. "Hey, honey," she said, sitting down beside him.

"I've noticed you've been looking exhausted lately. Are you feeling okay?"

Sam sighed, rubbing his face. "Honestly? I feel worn out. Work has been nonstop, and I just don't have the energy to do anything by the time I get home. I know I'm not taking care of myself the way I should, but I don't even know where to start."

Rachel nodded, her heart aching for him. "I get it. You've been working so hard, and I'm so grateful for everything you do for us. But I want you to be healthy, not just for me and the kids, but for you. I want you to feel strong and energized again. What if we started small? Maybe we could walk together in the evening, just to get out and clear our heads."

Sam hesitated but finally nodded. "That doesn't sound too bad. I think I could handle that."

The next evening, Rachel and Sam laced up their sneakers and headed out for a walk around the neighborhood after dinner. At first, Sam was reluctant, dragging his feet and joking about how he was "too old for this." But as they strolled and talked, Rachel noticed a change in his demeanor. He seemed more relaxed, smiling as they passed a group of kids playing basketball in a driveway. Sam admitted that by the time they got home, "That actually felt good. Thanks for getting me out of the house."

Over the next few weeks, their walks became a nightly routine. They used the time to talk about their day, their dreams, and even their struggles. Rachel saw how much these simple moments of connection meant to both of them, and she prayed daily for Sam's health, asking God to give him the strength and motivation to make positive changes.

Encouraged by the progress, Rachel suggested other small adjustments. They started cooking healthier meals together, experimenting with new recipes that the whole family enjoyed. Sam began packing lunches for work instead of relying on takeout, and Rachel noticed how much better he seemed to feel when he ate real food instead of fast food. She even bought him a fitness tracker as a small gift. To her surprise, Sam became excited about setting goals and tracking his progress.

One weekend, Sam decided to dust off his old bike and go for a ride with their son, Caleb. Watching them pedal off together, Rachel felt a surge of gratitude. Sam was finding joy in being active again, impacting their whole family. Caleb loved spending time with his dad, and even their daughter, Lily, started joining in on evening walks with Rachel and Sam.

A few months later, as Sam pulled on a jacket he hadn't worn in a while, Rachel saw him grin. "It's looser," he said proudly. "I haven't felt this good in years." Rachel smiled, wrapping her arms around him. "You've been doing amazing," she said. "I'm so proud of you."

That night, as Rachel lay in bed, she thanked God for the transformation she was witnessing. It wasn't just about Sam's physical health but his renewed energy, confidence, and joy. She realized that her prayers for him hadn't just been about fitness; they had been about asking God to restore her husband's spirit and remind him that his body was a temple of the Holy Spirit.

Over time, these small steps became a lifestyle for their family. They spent more time outdoors, cooking meals together and even planning weekend hikes and bike rides. Rachel was grateful for Sam's improved health and how these changes had drawn them closer as a family. It reminded her of God's faithfulness and His care for every aspect of their lives, including their physical well-being.

"Do you not know that your bodies are temples of the Holy Spirit, who is in you, whom you have received from God? You are not your own; you were bought at a price. Therefore honor God with your bodies." – 1 Corinthians 6:19-20 (NIV)

This verse reminds us that our physical bodies are sacred because they are temples of the Holy Spirit. As believers, we are entrusted with the responsibility to steward our spiritual lives and physical health as an act of worship and gratitude to God for the gift of life. Caring for our bodies isn't about achieving perfection but honoring God with how we use and care for what He has given us.

Sam's journey toward better health illustrates this principle beautifully. His decision to take small, consistent steps —like walking with Rachel, making healthier food choices, and finding joy in physical activity—revitalized his energy and confidence and deepened his connection with his family. His renewed health allowed him to fully engage in his role as a husband and father, creating opportunities to serve his family with greater impact and to enjoy moments with them that he might otherwise have missed.

When we prioritize our health, we open the door to greater availability for God's purposes in our lives. A healthy body allows us to serve more effectively, embrace ministry opportunities, and remain present for our loved ones for years to come. Whether playing with our children, joining a spouse on an outdoor adventure, or stepping up for a neighbor in need, our ability to engage fully is directly tied to how well we care for our physical selves.

This verse also reminds us that health's significance extends beyond the physical. When Sam improved his health, it brought vitality, joy, unity, and a renewed spirit to his household.

> A healthy body allows us to serve more effectively, embrace ministry opportunities, and remain present for our loved ones for years to come.

The nightly walks and shared meals strengthened his bond with Rachel and their children, showing how small acts of stewardship can ripple into blessings that impact an entire family.

Ultimately, caring for our health is not about striving for worldly standards but about worshiping God with our whole selves—body, mind, and spirit. As Rachel and Sam discovered, taking intentional steps to honor God through their physical health brought transformation to their lives, drawing them closer to each other and Him. This principle reminds us that when we honor God with our bodies, we invite His presence into every aspect of our lives, experiencing His faithfulness in ways that strengthen our health and our faith and relationships.

REFLECTION:

1. How can I encourage my husband to make healthy choices without sounding critical?

Am I modeling healthy habits in a way that inspires him rather than pressures him? How can I communicate care and concern in a supportive and not judgmental way?

2. Are there any small changes we could make together for better health?

What shared activities or goals could strengthen both our health and our relationship? How can I invite him to pursue wellness as a team effort?

3. How can I pray for his physical, mental, and emotional well-being?

Are there specific areas where he struggles or could use strength and encouragement? How can I commit to praying for him, asking for God's healing and renewal in every area of his life?

PRAYER:

"Lord, I thank you for my husband's health, and I pray for protection over his body. Guide him to make wise choices to stay strong and healthy. Help me to support and encourage him to take care of his body, which is a temple of your Spirit. Amen."

TODAY'S CALL TO ACTION:

Suggest one small, healthy activity you can do together—like a walk, preparing a meal, or planning a restful evening. Pray for his physical, mental, and emotional well-being.

Day 12

SELF-IMAGE

"...I am fearfully and wonderfully made."

Nate had always been confident and self-assured, but lately, Rachel noticed a shift. He seemed quieter, less enthusiastic, and often dismissed compliments with a self-deprecating comment. She first saw it when they were preparing for a rare date night. As Rachel adjusted her earrings in the mirror, she caught Nate frowning at his reflection. He tugged at his shirt, muttering, "I've really let myself go. I look like a dad from one of those sitcoms." Rachel laughed lightly, trying to ease the tension, but his shoulders remained slumped.

Over the following weeks, Rachel observed other signs of Nate's confidence waning. He avoided their usual gym visits, waved off her compliments about his appearance, and hesitated to speak up during a family gathering—a stark contrast to the man who once commanded the room with his humor and warmth. One night, as they sat together on the couch, she brought it up gently. "Nate, is everything okay? You've seemed a little down on yourself lately."

Nate sighed, staring at the coffee table. "I don't know. I guess I just feel like I'm not the man I used to be. I see pictures from a few years ago, and I can't believe how much I've changed. I'm not as fit, not as sharp at work. I feel like I'm just getting older and fading into the background."

Rachel's heart ached as she listened to him. She understood where he was coming from—life had been busy and stressful, with work demands and raising two teenagers. But she also knew that Nate was still the same incredible man she had fallen in love with, even if he couldn't see it right now. She prayed silently for the right words to encourage him.

"Nate," she began softly, turning toward him. "I wish you could see yourself the way I see you. You're more than your job performance or how you look in a picture. You're a man of integrity, strength, and kindness. The way you show up for me and the kids every single day—that's the real you. That's what matters."

Nate looked at her, his expression softening. "I guess it's just hard to shake this feeling," he admitted. "I feel like I've peaked, and now I'm just coasting."

Rachel reached for his hand. "You're not coasting, Nate. God's not done with you yet. He's still shaping you, and your worth isn't tied to how you look or what you achieve. It's tied to who you are in Him. Let me pray with you about this?"

Nate nodded, and Rachel prayed for him, asking God to remind Nate of his worth, to renew his confidence, and to help him see himself through God's eyes. She also prayed for her own heart, asking for the wisdom and grace to keep encouraging Nate in the days ahead.

Over the next few weeks, Rachel made a conscious effort to speak words of affirmation to Nate. She pointed out the things he did well, whether fixing something around the house, making their kids laugh, or handling a challenging situation at work with grace. Slowly, she noticed Nate beginning to regain some of his spark. He started opening up more, even cracking jokes about his "dad bod." He also joined her again on their evening walks.

One Saturday morning, as Nate worked on a project in the garage, Rachel heard laughter coming from inside. She peeked in and saw their son, Tyler, intently listening as Nate taught him how to use a power drill. Nate was fully engaged, explaining everything with enthusiasm and confidence. Rachel couldn't help but smile, seeing glimpses of the man Nate had rediscovered himself to be—a strong, capable, and loving father.

A few months later, during a quiet moment after dinner, Nate turned to Rachel and said, "I've been thinking about what you said that night. About God not being done with me. It really stuck with me. I'm starting to believe it, too. I don't have to be the same guy I was ten years ago to be worth something."

Rachel felt tears well up in her eyes as she nodded. "You've always been worth everything to me," she said. "And to God."

This journey reminded Rachel of how powerful her words and prayers could be in building Nate up. For Nate, it was a season of learning that his identity wasn't tied to his appearance or achievements but to who he was as a husband, father, and child of God. Together, they discovered that true self-worth comes not from the world's standards but from the unwavering love and value God places on each of us.

> "For you created my inmost being;
> you knit me together in my mother's womb.
> I praise you because I am fearfully and
> wonderfully made;
> your works are wonderful,
> I know that full well.
> My frame was not hidden from you
> when I was made in the secret place,
> when I was woven together in the depths of
> the earth.
> Your eyes saw my unformed body;
> all the days ordained for me were written in
> your book
> before one of them came to be."
> – Psalm 139:13-16 (NIV)

This verse highlights the intimate care and intentionality with which God created each of us. It reminds us that our worth and identity are rooted not in external achievements, appearances, or the opinions of others but in the truth that we are created by God in His image. Recognizing that we are "fearfully and wonderfully made" should lead us to worship God for His craftsmanship and find confidence in His design.

Nate's struggle with his self-image reveals the pressures many people face—whether it's dissatisfaction with physical changes, feelings of inadequacy at work, or comparisons to others. This verse speaks directly to Nate's need to shift his focus from worldly standards to God's truth. As he learns to see himself through God's eyes, he begins to embrace the unique value and purpose God has placed in him.

This verse's application is transformative. It invites us to reject the lies of insecurity, comparison, and self-doubt and rest in the assurance that we are created with care and purpose. By praising God for how He made us, we not only honor Him but also align our self-perception with His truth.

For Nate, embracing this perspective restores his confidence. It renews his ability to fulfill his roles as a husband, father, and child of God. It also impacts his relationships, as his newfound peace allows him to engage with others authentically and with joy.

> By praising God for how He made us, we not only honor Him but also align our self-perception with His truth.

This verse challenges all believers to treat themselves—and others—as God's unique and beloved creations. It reminds us that when we see ourselves as "fearfully and wonderfully made," we glorify the Creator and walk in the identity He has lovingly given us.

If your husband struggles with self-worth, whether due to his faith journey or life circumstances, pray that God would reveal his unique value as a beloved child of God. Your affirmations and encouragement can reflect God's truth to him.

REFLECTION:

1. Are there ways I can help my husband feel confident and valued?

Do my words and actions consistently affirm his worth and contributions? How can I intentionally build him up, especially when he might feel inadequate or unseen?

2. Do I notice and affirm his strengths and gifts often?

Am I specific in pointing out the unique qualities and talents God has given him? How can I reflect gratitude for who he is, not just for what he does?

3. How can I pray for him to see himself as God sees him, worthy and loved?

Are there lies or insecurities he might believe about himself that I can address in prayer? How can I intercede for him to experience God's love and truth in a transformative way?

PRAYER:

"God, I lift up my husband's self-image to you. Remind him that he is fearfully and wonderfully made. Help him to see himself as you see him, full of worth and purpose. Let him know that his value is rooted in Christ, not accomplishments or appearance. Amen."

TODAY'S CALL TO ACTION:

Speak a word of encouragement to your husband about a quality or accomplishment you admire. Pray that God will help him see himself as "fearfully and wonderfully made."

Day 13

COURAGE

"Be strong and courageous."

Brian had always been a steady, dependable husband
and father. He wasn't the kind of man who made
impulsive decisions or took unnecessary risks, which Megan
loved about him. But there was one thing she wished she
could help him overcome: his hesitation to step outside his
comfort zone when opportunities arose. Over the years,
Megan had seen Brian pass up chances to lead at work, join
community projects, or pursue hobbies he had always
discussed. His default response was, "I'm just not that kind
of guy," or, "What if I fail?"

One evening, Megan saw an announcement for a local
church initiative—a mentoring program for at-risk youth. The
church sought men to mentor middle and high school boys

who lacked father figures. As soon as Megan read it, she thought of Brian. He had always been great with their kids, and she'd seen how young men at church naturally gravitated toward him, drawn to his quiet wisdom and steady presence.

"Hey, Brian," she said, handing him the flyer after dinner. "I think you'd be amazing at this."

Brian glanced at the flyer, his brow furrowing. "A mentor?" he asked, setting it down. "I don't know, Meg. I mean, I wouldn't even know where to start. What if I say the wrong thing? What if I don't connect with the kid?"

Megan smiled, sliding into the chair beside him. "You already mentor our kids every single day," she said. "And you do it without even thinking about it. You have so much to offer, Brian—your kindness, integrity, love for God. You don't have to be perfect; you just have to show up."

Brian shrugged, clearly unsure. "It's a big responsibility," he said quietly. "What if I let the kid down?"

Megan reached for his hand. "You won't," she said firmly. "And even if you feel like you're not enough, God is. This isn't about being perfect; it's about trusting Him to use you just as you are. Maybe this is exactly the kind of thing God is calling you to."

That night, Megan prayed for Brian, asking God to give him the courage to step into something new and to trust that he had what it took to make a difference. She didn't push him, knowing he needed time to think and pray about it alone.

Over the next week, Megan noticed Brian rereading the flyer. Once, she overheard him on the phone with a friend from church, asking questions about the program. She prayed quietly, trusting God to work in Brian's heart.

A week later, Brian surprised her by saying, "I signed up for the mentoring program." Megan's eyes lit up. "Really? That's amazing!" she said. Brian smiled sheepishly. "I'm still nervous, but I figure if God's asking me to do this, He'll help me figure it out."

Over the next few months, Brian regularly met with Marcus, a 14-year-old boy from a single-parent home. At first, the meetings were awkward, with Marcus responding in one-word answers and Brian unsure of what to say. But Brian stuck with it, showing up with an open heart every week. Gradually, Marcus began to open up, sharing stories about his struggles at school and his dreams of becoming an engineer. Brian listened intently, offering encouragement and advice when he could.

One day, as they worked on a model car together, Marcus looked up and said, "You know, I've never had anyone take time for me like this. I didn't think I'd like having a mentor, but I'm glad you're here." Brian felt a lump in his throat, realizing that his simple willingness to show up had already made an impact.

At home, Megan saw a transformation in Brian. He seemed more confident, more purposeful, and even more engaged with their own kids. "I think this mentoring thing is teaching me as much as it's teaching Marcus," he admitted one evening. "I didn't think I had what it took, but God keeps showing me that it's not about being perfect—it's about being willing."

For Megan, watching Brian step into this role was a testament to the power of prayer and encouragement. For Brian, it was a reminder that courage isn't the absence of fear—it's choosing to trust God in the face of it. Together, they marveled at how God could use small acts of faith to create lasting change, not just in Marcus's life but also in the life of their family.

> "Be strong and courageous. Do not be afraid; do not be discouraged, for the Lord your God will be with you wherever you go." – Joshua 1:9 (NIV)

> **Courage is not the absence of fear but the willingness to act in obedience, trusting God to handle what we cannot.**

This verse is a powerful reminder of God's presence and faithfulness, especially in moments of uncertainty and fear. Spoken to Joshua as he prepared to lead Israel into the Promised Land, it calls for courage not based on self-reliance but on the assurance that God is with us. It's a promise that wherever God calls us, His presence and strength will equip us to face challenges with confidence.

Brian's reluctance to mentor reflects a common struggle: the fear of inadequacy and failure. This verse directly speaks to his situation, encouraging him to move forward, not because he feels ready or equipped, but because God's presence will empower him. By stepping into his role as a mentor despite his fears, Brian learns to trust God's promise that He will provide the strength to accomplish His purposes.

This verse applies to all believers. It challenges us to step out in faith, even when we feel unprepared, knowing that God is not only with us but also working through us. In this context, courage is not the absence of fear but the willingness to act in obedience, trusting God to handle what we cannot.

For Brian, embracing this truth allows him to make an impact far beyond what he imagined, as his obedience inspires and blesses others. For all of us, this verse serves as a foundation for bold, faith-filled action in our everyday lives, reminding us that we can face any challenge with confidence because we are never alone.

If your husband feels reluctant to lead or unsure of how to step into this role, be comforted in knowing that God's design for leadership is not about perfection but faithfulness. Be patient. Your gentle encouragement and prayers can create an atmosphere where he feels safe to grow, knowing he is loved and supported no matter where he starts.

REFLECTION:

1. Are there specific fears or challenges he's facing now where he needs courage?

Am I aware of the fears or uncertainties weighing on his heart? How can I offer encouragement and point him to God's promises to strengthen his confidence?

2. How can I show him that I'm a safe place to share his fears?

Do my words and reactions create an environment where he feels secure opening up about his struggles? How can I intentionally show grace and understanding when he is vulnerable?

3. What prayers of courage and confidence can I pray over him today?

Are there specific areas of his life—work, relationships, or personal growth—where he needs God's strength? How can I declare God's promises over him in prayer to remind him that he is never alone?

PRAYER:

"Heavenly Father, give my husband the courage to face life's challenges with faith and determination. Let him trust in you even when things are uncertain. I pray he will be strong and courageous, knowing you are by his side, guiding him every step of the way. Amen."

TODAY'S CALL TO ACTION:

Encourage your husband to take one small step toward a
challenge or goal he may feel hesitant about. Pray for his
courage and confidence in trusting God's guidance.

Day 14

MOTIVATION

"The one who is unwilling to work shall not eat."

Laura loved her husband, Ethan, deeply. Still, over the years, she had become increasingly concerned about his lack of motivation with regard to work and providing for their family. They had been married for three years, and Ethan was a kind, creative, and compassionate man. Still, he struggled to find his footing professionally. Ethan had bounced between jobs since college, often leaving positions when they became challenging or unfulfilling. He was between jobs again, spending his days at home with no clear plan for what was next.

Laura tried to be understanding. She knew the job market was tough, and Ethan wanted to find something he was passionate about. However, the weight of being the primary provider was starting to wear on her, emotionally and financially. She had taken on extra hours at work to make ends meet. She couldn't help but feel resentful when she came home to see Ethan still in his pajamas, scrolling through job postings but not following through.

One evening, after a long day at work, Laura sat on the couch next to Ethan. "How's the job search going?" she asked, trying to keep her tone light.

Ethan sighed, setting his phone down. "I don't know," he said. "I've looked at a few things, but nothing feels right. I just don't want to end up in another dead-end job."

Laura bit her lip, choosing her words carefully. "I get that," she said. "But we can't afford for you to wait forever. I know you're looking for something you'll love, but maybe the right job isn't going to feel perfect at first. It might just be the one that provides for us right now and opens doors for the future."

Ethan frowned, leaning back in his chair. "I just feel stuck," he admitted. "Like nothing I do is going to make a difference. What's the point?"

Laura's heart broke hearing his frustration. She had been praying for Ethan for weeks, asking God to stir up his motivation and help him find a sense of purpose. That night, after Ethan had gone to bed, Laura stayed up, pouring her heart out to God. "Lord, please help Ethan see the gifts you've given him. Help him find work that fulfills himself and honors You, and give him the courage to take the first step, even if it's not perfect."

The following day, Laura woke up determined to

encourage Ethan rather than push him. "Hey," she said over breakfast, "I've been thinking. You've always been great at fixing things and working with your hands. Have you ever thought about looking into something like carpentry or maintenance work? It might not be forever, but it could be a good start."

Ethan was quiet for a moment, then nodded. "I guess I've never really considered that," he said. "I've always liked working on stuff like that."

Encouraged by his response, Laura found a local job fair happening the following week and suggested they check it out together. At first, Ethan was reluctant, but with her support, he agreed to go. At the fair, Ethan met a small business owner looking for someone to apprentice in carpentry. The role wasn't glamorous, but it offered steady work, a chance to learn new skills, and opportunities for growth. Ethan hesitated but decided to apply.

Over the next few months, Laura saw a transformation in Ethan. The job wasn't easy, and there were days when he came home exhausted and frustrated, but he stuck with it. Slowly, his confidence grew as he mastered new skills and received positive feedback from his employer. For the first time in years, Ethan seemed proud of his work.

One evening, as they sat together on the porch, Ethan turned to Laura. "You know, I wasn't sure about this job at first, but it's been good for me," he said. "It feels good to come home knowing I've done something productive. Thanks for not giving up on me."

Laura smiled, her heart full of gratitude. "I never gave up on you, Ethan," she said. "And God hasn't either. I've been praying for you every step of the way, and I'm so proud of you for taking this leap."

This journey reminded Laura of the importance of prayer, patience, and gentle encouragement. It taught Ethan to trust God with the process and find purpose in the work before him. Together, they saw how taking small steps of faith could lead to growth, stability, and renewed motivation for the future.

For even when we were with you, we gave you this rule: "The one who is unwilling to work shall not eat." We hear that some among you are idle and disruptive. They are not busy; they are busybodies. Such people we command and urge in the Lord Jesus Christ to settle down and earn the food they eat. – 2 Thessalonians 3:10-12 (NIV)

This passage directly addresses the importance of diligence and responsibility in work. Paul exhorts believers to reject idleness and contribute meaningfully to their sustenance and community. The call to "settle down and earn the food they eat" reflects God's design for work as both a blessing and a responsibility, emphasizing that work honors God and supports the well-being of individuals and families.

Ethan's lack of motivation and tendency to drift between jobs mirror the warning in this passage. When he takes initiative and pursues steady work, he aligns himself with the biblical principle of diligence. His decision to stop waiting for the "perfect opportunity" and commit to purposeful action demonstrates obedience to this command. It brings stability and growth to his family.

Every marriage has seasons —times of joy and unity and times of struggle and distance. If you find yourself in a season where your husband seems

> **Work is necessary and a God-given means of provision and stewardship.**

disengaged or uncertain about his path, know that God is near. He sees your heart and hears your prayers, even when progress feels slow. Your role is not to carry the burden of change alone but to trust in God's ability to work in your husband's heart and circumstances. Loving steadfastly through this season reflects God's faithfulness and invites His transformative work into your marriage.

This verse's application is deeply practical. It reminds believers that work is necessary and a God-given means of provision and stewardship. While work can be challenging or mundane, embracing it with a heart of obedience reflects faithfulness to God's design. Ethan's transformation shows how diligence honors God and fosters personal and spiritual growth.

For all believers, this passage reminds us that idleness is not neutral—it can disrupt lives and relationships. Instead, God calls us to live purposefully, contributing to our families and communities through meaningful effort. When we work in obedience and trust, we reflect God's character and experience His provision in powerful ways.

REFLECTION:

1. How can I inspire him to pursue his goals without pressuring him?

Am I encouraging his dreams in a way that fuels his confidence, or do I unintentionally add to his stress? How can I affirm his efforts and remind him that small steps of progress matter?

2. Are there practical ways I can help him feel motivated and encouraged?

What specific actions or words of affirmation could I offer to reignite his sense of purpose? How can I work alongside him to remove obstacles that might be holding him back?

3. How can I pray for his energy and enthusiasm, especially in seasons of weariness?

Are there areas where he seems discouraged or overwhelmed? How can I pray for God to refresh his spirit, renew his focus, and restore his joy in pursuing his calling?

PRAYER:

"God, stir up initiative and motivation in my husband's heart. Help him to be diligent and passionate about the work you've called him to do. Let him be inspired to pursue his goals with confidently and joyfully, always honoring you in his efforts. Amen."

TODAY'S CALL TO ACTION:

Offer a gentle reminder of a goal or passion your husband has previously mentioned, encouraging him to revisit it. Commit to praying for renewed energy and enthusiasm in his pursuits.

Day 15

<hr />

FRIENDSHIPS / HIS CIRCLE OF 5

"...a companion of fools suffers harm."

Megan had always heard the saying, "You become like the five people you spend the most time with." While she wasn't sure if that was completely true, she had begun to notice how much her husband, Ryan, was influenced by the people around him. Ryan was naturally friendly and had a knack for connecting with others, but lately, Megan had started to wonder if some of his closest friendships were having a negative impact on him.

Ryan had a group of buddies from college he still kept in touch with, and while Megan liked most of them, there were a couple of guys in the group whose values didn't align with hers... or Ryan's. Whenever Ryan hung out with them, she noticed subtle changes in his behavior. He came home more irritable, more dismissive of their family priorities, and less motivated to engage in their shared faith. Megan wasn't sure how to bring it up without sounding judgmental or overbearing, so instead, she prayed. "Lord, help Ryan to see who in his life lifts him up and who pulls him down. Surround him with godly friends who will encourage and strengthen him."

One Friday night, as Ryan got ready to go out with his friends, Megan hesitated before speaking. "Hey, Ryan," she said gently. "Have you ever thought about how much the people we spend time with influence us? I know your friends mean a lot to you, but I wonder if some of them encourage the best version of you."

Ryan looked at her, surprised. "What do you mean?" he asked.

Megan chose her words carefully. "I think about how you're always so energized and focused after you spend time with guys like Jake from church. But sometimes, after you hang out with Matt and Brad, you seem...off. Not quite yourself."

Ryan frowned, considering her words. "I guess I hadn't really thought about it that way," he admitted. "But maybe you're right. I do feel like I'm trying to keep up with them sometimes."

Megan nodded, encouraged by his openness. "I'm not saying you should cut anyone out of your life," she said. "But maybe it's worth thinking about who's helping you grow and who might be holding you back."

Over the next few weeks, Megan prayed specifically for Ryan to seek out friendships that would help him grow spiritually and emotionally. She also encouraged him to reconnect with Jake, a fellow dad from their church who had always been a positive influence on Ryan. When Jake invited Ryan to join a men's group, Ryan was hesitant at first, worried it might feel too formal or awkward. But after some gentle nudging from Megan, he agreed to give it a try.

To Ryan's surprise, the men's group quickly became a highlight of his week. The group was a mix of guys in different stages of life, and their discussions were honest, practical, and focused on growing in their faith. Ryan found himself opening up in ways he hadn't expected, sharing his struggles and receiving encouragement from men who understood what he was going through. He began to feel a renewed sense of purpose and direction.

One Saturday afternoon, as Ryan and Megan sat in the backyard watching their kids play, Ryan turned to her. "You were right," he said. "I didn't realize how much some of my friendships were weighing me down. Being around these guys from church—it's different. They challenge me to be better, but they also remind me that I don't have to have it all figured out."

Megan smiled, feeling a wave of gratitude. "I've been praying for you," she said. "I knew God would bring the right people into your life."

Over time, Ryan began to shift his priorities. While he still kept in touch with his old friends, he spent less time with those who weren't helping him grow and more time building relationships that inspired and encouraged him. He even started organizing get-togethers with the men from his group, inviting others to join and experience the same support he had found.

For Megan, this journey was a reminder of the importance of praying for her husband's relationships and trusting God to guide him. For Ryan, it was a powerful lesson in the impact of community and the value of surrounding himself with people who encouraged him to become the man God was calling him to be. Together, they saw how a godly circle of friends could not only strengthen Ryan but also bless their family as a whole.

"Walk with the wise and become wise, for a companion of fools suffers harm." – Proverbs 13:20 (NIV)

Proverbs emphasizes the profound influence our closest relationships have on our lives. Walking with wise people—those who live with integrity, seek God's guidance, and demonstrate good character—leads to growth, wisdom, and blessings. Conversely, surrounding ourselves with unwise or foolish companions can lead to harm, poor decisions, and spiritual stagnation.

Ryan's struggle with his circle of friends illustrates this truth. While he values his college buddies, he begins to recognize how some of them pull him away from the man God is calling him to be. His decision to spend more time with godly friends demonstrates the transformative power of wise relationships. These new friendships challenge him to grow in his faith, develop better habits, and prioritize his role as a husband and father.

The application of this verse challenges believers to evaluate their inner circle. Are the people we spend the most time with encouraging us in our walk with God, or are they leading us into harmful patterns? Ryan's story

> Walking with wise people —those who live with integrity, seek God's guidance, and demonstrate good character—leads to growth, wisdom, and blessings.

shows that by intentionally choosing friends who live wisely and honor God, we can become more like Christ and strengthen our families and communities.

This verse also reminds us of the responsibility we carry as friends. Just as wise friends influence us for good, we are called to be that influence for others. Ryan's journey inspires us to cultivate friendships that uplift, sharpen, and encourage one another toward God's best for our lives. Surrounding ourselves with wise companions is not just about protecting ourselves—it's about fulfilling God's design for community and mutual edification.

REFLECTION:

1. Are there people in his life who help him grow spiritually?

Am I intentional about encouraging his relationships with friends who uplift and inspire him? How can I pray for God to deepen those connections and bring more godly influences into his life? What about me, what people do I have in my life that help me grow spiritually?

2. How can I support him in forming strong, positive friendships?

Are there ways I can create opportunities for him to spend time with men who share his values? How can I affirm the importance of these friendships in shaping his growth and character?

3. What can I pray over his closest friendships to bring godly influence and support?

Are there specific relationships where he needs wisdom or discernment? How can I pray for his friendships to reflect God's love and truth, encouraging him to walk faithfully in his calling?

PRAYER:

"Lord, thank you for the friendships in our lives. Surround my husband with godly men who encourage and strengthen him. Let his closest friends be those who point him to you, and help him to be a positive influence in his circle. Amen."

TODAY'S CALL TO ACTION:

Affirm one positive influence in your husband's life and thank God for that relationship. Pray for wisdom in cultivating friendships that encourage his spiritual and emotional growth.

Day 16

INFLUENCE

"Let your light shine..."

David had always been a quiet man who preferred to let his actions speak louder than his words. He wasn't the kind to command attention in a room or offer unsolicited advice. Still, Megan had long admired his steady integrity and thoughtfulness. Over the years, she had seen countless people come to David for guidance, drawn to his calm demeanor and sound judgment. But David didn't seem to realize just how much influence he had.

One evening, as they were finishing dinner, Megan mentioned a conversation she had overheard at church. A young couple had been talking about David, praising how he had encouraged them during a challenging season. "They said your advice helped them figure out how to navigate their finances without losing sight of their faith," Megan shared.

David looked up from his plate, surprised. "Really? I didn't think I said anything special. I just told them what I've learned along the way."

Megan smiled. "That's exactly why they respect you. You don't try to impress anyone or act like you have all the answers. You're just real, and people trust that."

David shrugged, clearly uncomfortable with the attention. "I don't know," he said. "I just do what I can."

But Megan saw something David didn't seem to see himself: his influence extended far beyond what he realized. Whether mentoring younger men at church, helping a neighbor fix their car, or showing patience and kindness at work, David's consistent faithfulness left a lasting impact on everyone around him. Megan often prayed that David would begin to see his influence as a gift from God and step into that role with more confidence and intentionality.

A few weeks later, an opportunity arose to test David's willingness to embrace his influence. Their pastor approached him after church one Sunday, asking if he would consider leading a small group for young married couples. "You have so much wisdom to offer," the pastor said. "And I know people would benefit from hearing your perspective."

David hesitated, unsure. "I'm not sure I'm the right person for that," he said. "I'm not a great speaker, and I don't know if I have anything new to share."

Megan, who had been standing nearby, stepped in. "You'd be perfect for this," she said. "You've been through so much and always trusted God through it all. Your testimony is exactly what people need to hear."

After much prayer and encouragement, David reluctantly agreed to lead the group. On the first night, he was nervous, stumbling over his words and second-guessing himself. But as the weeks went by, he began to grow more comfortable. The couples in the group opened up to him, sharing their struggles and seeking his advice. David found himself sharing stories from his own life—mistakes he had made, lessons he had learned, and ways God had been faithful through it all. To his surprise, people were deeply moved by his honesty and vulnerability.

One night, as the group wrapped up, a young man named Jake pulled David aside. "I just wanted to say thank you," Jake said. "Hearing how you and Megan worked through your challenges has given me hope. I've been struggling to lead my family, but you've shown me that it's okay to take it one step at a time."

David nodded, feeling a lump in his throat. "I'm glad it helped," he said.

As David and Megan sat on the porch that evening, he turned to her. "You were right," he admitted. "I didn't think I had much to offer, but God's been using me in ways I didn't expect. It's humbling, but knowing I'm making a difference feels good."

Megan smiled, squeezing his hand. "You've always had that influence, David. Now you're just letting God use it."

For David, this journey was a reminder that influence

doesn't always come with a platform or a title. It comes from living faithfully, treating others with kindness, and being willing to share the lessons God has taught you. It was a joy for Megan to see David step into his God-given role as a mentor and leader, knowing his quiet faithfulness was impacting lives in ways they might never fully see.

> *"...let your light shine before others, that they may see your good deeds and glorify your Father in heaven." –* *Matthew 5:16 (NIV)*

The apostle Matthew calls believers to live in a way that reflects God's goodness so others are drawn to Him. It emphasizes that influence isn't about personal recognition but pointing people to God through our actions, character, and choices.

> **When surrendered to God, influence becomes a powerful testimony of His love and grace.**

In this story, David's humility causes him to underestimate the impact of his steady faithfulness. Yet, through his interactions with coworkers, neighbors, and his family, he begins to see how his actions inspire others. By stepping into leadership at church, he realizes that influence is about showing Christ's love in everyday moments, not about being perfect or loud.

This verse reminds believers that our lives are constantly influencing those around us. Through kindness, patience, or quiet strength, we can reflect God's light in ways that encourage and inspire others. Living intentionally with humility and faithfulness allows God to work through us, drawing others to glorify Him. When surrendered to God, influence becomes a powerful testimony of His love and grace.

Not all influence is positive, and there may be times when your husband's choices or actions seem to have a negative or ungodly impact on those around him. This can be discouraging, especially if you long to see Christ's love reflected through him. Remember that God is still at work in these moments, even when the transformation feels distant.

Begin by praying specifically for areas where his influence may be misaligned with God's will. Ask God to reveal His truth to your husband in ways that only He can. Pray for wisdom to discern when to speak and when to remain silent, trusting that God is working in your husband's heart.

If the timing feels right, gently and lovingly share your observations with him. Focus on how his influence could align with the qualities you know God has given him—his kindness, strength, or integrity. Instead of focusing on the negative, speak to his potential and how God can use him powerfully for good.

For example, you might say, "*I've seen how much people look up to you, and I know God has given you so much wisdom to share. I think He has even greater plans for using your influence to bless others.*" This approach affirms his value while planting seeds for reflection and growth.

Remember, change is ultimately God's work. Your role is

to pray, love, and encourage, trusting that God can redeem and redirect any influence toward His purposes. Just as David realized his quiet faithfulness was a powerful testimony, your husband can learn to let God use him to shine His light.

REFLECTION:

1. How can I encourage him to use his influence to honor God at home and beyond?

Am I recognizing and affirming the ways he already positively impacts others? How can I encourage him to lean into his unique strengths and trust God to use him as a light in his relationships and community?

2. Are there opportunities for influence that he might feel hesitant about?

Do I notice areas where he feels unsure or inadequate in stepping into leadership or mentorship roles? How can I lovingly support and pray for him to embrace these opportunities with courage and faith?

3. What can I pray for regarding his leadership and witness to others?

What specific roles or relationships could benefit from God's guidance in shaping his influence? How can I intercede for his leadership to reflect Christ's humility, wisdom, and love?

PRAYER:

"Father, I pray for my husband's influence to reflect you. Help him to be a role model to others, especially within our family. Let his words and actions show your love and grace to everyone he meets, bringing others closer to you.
Lord, I lift up my husband's influence to You. If there are areas where his choices or actions do not reflect Your love, I ask for Your gentle conviction and guidance in his life. Help him see the impact of his words and actions and surrender those areas to You. Equip me with wisdom and grace to lovingly support him as You work in his heart. Use his life to glorify You and draw others closer to You. Amen."

TODAY'S CALL TO ACTION:

Recognize a moment when your husband's actions or words positively influenced others, and tell him how much it means. Pray for his continued impact as a godly example.

Day 17

INTIMACY

"...his desire is for me."

Emma and Jake had been married for almost ten years. With two young kids, demanding jobs, and the busyness of life, their marriage had shifted over the years. What had once been a vibrant and passionate connection had faded into a routine rhythm. Between managing their schedules, caring for the kids, and juggling household responsibilities, physical intimacy had become an afterthought.

Emma felt the growing distance between them, but she wasn't sure how to address it. She noticed Jake seemed more withdrawn lately, spending more time on his phone in the evenings or zoning out in front of the TV. She, too, was exhausted, often falling into bed with barely enough energy to pray, let alone connect with her husband. It wasn't that they didn't love each other, they did. But the spark that had once drawn them together seemed buried under the weight of daily life.

One evening, after putting the kids to bed, Emma sat quietly on the couch, thinking about their relationship. She longed for the closeness they had shared in their early years of marriage—not just physical intimacy but the emotional and spiritual connection that had made them feel like a team. She prayed silently, asking God for wisdom and guidance. "Lord, I know intimacy is your gift to us as husband and wife, but we've lost something along the way. Help us to rebuild that connection and honor You in this part of our marriage."

That weekend, Emma decided to start small. While Jake was working on a project in the garage, she brought him a cup of coffee and asked if she could sit with him. He looked up, surprised but pleased. "Of course," he said, setting down his tools. They talked about his project, the kids, and a funny memory from their honeymoon. It was the first time in weeks they had shared a conversation that wasn't about logistics or responsibilities.

Encouraged by this small moment, Emma began looking for other ways to reconnect with Jake. One day, she left him a note in his lunchbox, simply saying, "I'm so grateful for you." That evening, Jake mentioned it with a smile. "I needed that today," he said.

Slowly, their conversations grew deeper, and they began to carve out time for each other. One night, after the kids were asleep, Emma suggested they play a board game—

something they used to do before life got so hectic. Jake laughed, saying, "I haven't played this in years," but he joined in, and they spent the evening laughing like they hadn't in ages. It reminded both of them of the joy they'd once shared so easily.

As their emotional connection deepened, Emma felt God nudging her to discuss their physical intimacy. One evening, as they were lying in bed, she turned to Jake and said, "Can I share something with you?" He nodded, looking curious. "I feel like we've been drifting apart, and I miss being close to you—not just emotionally, but physically too. I know life's been crazy, but I want us to prioritize this part of our marriage again."

Jake looked thoughtful, then reached for her hand. "I've been feeling that too," he admitted. "I guess I didn't know how to bring it up. I've been so stressed with work and everything, but you're right—we need to work on this together."

That conversation marked a turning point for Emma and Jake. They began to be more intentional about their physical intimacy, not seeing it as just another task on their to-do list but as a way to deepen their bond and express their love for each other. They also prayed together, asking God to bless this area of their marriage and to help them honor Him through their love for each other.

Over time, Emma and Jake rediscovered the joy and passion they had once shared. They realized that intimacy wasn't just about physical connection but about creating a safe space where they could be fully known and loved. They started planning regular date nights, even if it was just an hour together after the kids were asleep, and they worked to communicate openly about their needs and desires.

One evening, as they sat together on the couch, Jake said to Emma, "Thank you for not giving up on us. I didn't realize how much I needed this… how much I needed you."

Emma smiled, tears filling her eyes. "I didn't give up because I love you," she said. "And because I know this is what God wants for us. He brought us together and is helping us rebuild what we thought we'd lost."

For Emma and Jake, this journey was a reminder that intimacy is a gift from God that requires care, effort, and intentionality to keep alive. It wasn't always easy, but they found that as they prioritized each other and invited God into this part of their marriage, their love grew stronger than ever

"I am my beloved's, and his desire is for me." – Song of Solomon 7:10 (AMP)

The Song of Solomon beautifully celebrates the intimacy and mutual desire between a husband and wife as a gift from God. It reminds us that marital intimacy is not merely physical but emotional and spiritual, reflecting the covenantal love God designed for marriage. In a Christ-centered marriage, this verse highlights the importance of honoring and nurturing the bond that fosters connection, trust, and unity.

Emma and Jake's relationship reflects the challenges

many couples face in maintaining intimacy amidst the busyness of life. Over time, distractions, exhaustion, and unspoken frustrations can create distance. Still, this verse encourages couples to reclaim the beauty and joy of their God-given connection. Jake and Emma's intentional efforts to prioritize their physical and emotional intimacy align with God's design for marriage as a place of mutual delight and desire.

The application of this verse is twofold. First, it encourages couples to see intimacy as a sacred part of their marriage, not just a physical act but a deep expression of love and unity. By

> **God designed intimacy to be a joyful and integral part of marriage. This gift fosters closeness and reflects God's covenantal love for us.**

intentionally cultivating this connection, couples strengthen their relationship and reflect God's desire for oneness in marriage. Second, it reminds couples that intimacy thrives in mutual love, respect, and trust—qualities that require effort, communication, and prayer.

For Jake and Emma, rediscovering intimacy involves making time for each other, being vulnerable, and inviting God into this aspect of their marriage.

For all married couples, this verse reminds them that God designed intimacy to be a joyful and integral part of marriage. This gift fosters closeness and reflects God's covenantal love for us. By prioritizing this connection, couples honor God's purpose for their relationship and grow stronger together.

Intimacy may differ depending on your marriage season

or your husband's openness to connection. Trust that God can restore and nurture closeness in ways that reflect His design for your relationship.

REFLECTION:

1. How can I foster an atmosphere of trust and connection in our marriage?

Are there ways I can prioritize emotional safety and open communication to deepen our intimacy? How can I nurture an environment where he feels valued and fully known?

2. Do I regularly communicate my appreciation for him, physically and emotionally?

Am I intentional about expressing gratitude for the ways in which he loves and supports me? How can I show appreciation in ways that resonate with him both emotionally and physically?

3. How can I pray for a marriage relationship that honors God through mutual love and respect?

What specific areas of our connection—physical, emotional, or spiritual—can I lift up in prayer? How can I ask God to help us grow in unity and passion as a reflection of His design for marriage?

PRAYER:

"God, I thank You for the intimacy we share as husband and wife, a gift You designed to reflect Your covenantal love. Help us to grow closer, cherishing and respecting each other in every aspect of our relationship. Protect our marriage from distractions, misunderstandings, and anything that seeks to create distance between us. Teach us to communicate openly and lovingly, to prioritize time for one another, and to create an environment where trust and connection can thrive. Let our relationship honor You and be a testimony of Your love and faithfulness. Guide us in building trust, unity, and love, and help us to delight in the bond You have given us. Amen."

TODAY'S CALL TO ACTION:

Do one intentional thing to nurture intimacy. Ideas might include initiating a meaningful conversation, planning a date night, or expressing affection. Pray for God to deepen your connection.

Day 18

MARRIAGE

"A cord of three strands is not quickly broken."

A bby and Jake had been married for 12 years. They loved each other deeply, but lately, their marriage felt more like a business partnership than a love story. Between Jake's demanding job, Abby's responsibilities as a stay-at-home mom to their three kids, and the endless list of bills, appointments, and errands, their connection seemed to have taken a back seat. They rarely argued, but that was because they seldom talked about anything other than logistics. Abby couldn't remember the last time they had an actual date, and she often felt like they were living parallel lives under the same roof.

One evening, as Abby folded laundry on the couch, she noticed Jake sitting at the kitchen table, staring blankly at his laptop. He looked as tired as she felt. She sighed, longing for the days when they would spend hours talking about their dreams or laughing until their sides hurt. But those days felt like a distant memory.

That night, as Abby lay in bed, she couldn't shake the feeling that their marriage needed more. She whispered a prayer into the quiet. "Lord, You know we love each other, but we're stuck in a rut. Please help us find our way back to each other. Show me how to love Jake the way You want me to, and help us to make our marriage a priority again."

The following day, Abby decided to take a small step. She left a sticky note on Jake's coffee mug that read, "I'm thankful for you. You're a great husband and father." It was a simple gesture, but when Jake saw it, his face softened. "Thanks for this," he said, holding up the note. "I needed that today."

Encouraged by Jake's response, Abby continued looking for ways to show him she cared. She started asking him about his day and really listening instead of multitasking while he talked. She texted him little messages during the day, like, "Thinking of you. Can't wait to see you tonight." Jake began to respond in kind, sending her notes like, "I miss you. Let's plan a date soon."

A few weeks later, Abby decided to take things a step further. One evening, after the kids were in bed, she turned to Jake and said, "I miss us. I miss spending time together, just the two of us. Can we plan a date night soon?"

Jake looked up, surprised. "I miss us too," he admitted. "I've been so caught up with work and everything else that I guess I didn't realize how much we've drifted. Let's do it."

That Friday, Jake surprised Abby by arranging a babysitter and taking her to their favorite restaurant. Over dinner, they talked about everything and nothing, laughing like they hadn't in years. Abby felt her heart swell with gratitude. It wasn't just the date—it was the effort Jake was making and the connection they were beginning to rebuild.

Over the next few months, Abby and Jake made a point to prioritize their marriage. They started setting aside one evening a week as "their time," even if it was just sitting on the couch with a bowl of popcorn and a good movie after the kids were asleep. They also began praying together, something they hadn't done consistently since the early days of their marriage. At first, it felt awkward, but soon, it became one of the most meaningful parts of their week.

One evening, as they sat on the porch watching the sunset, Jake turned to Abby and said, "You know, I didn't realize how much we needed this—how much I needed this. Thank you for not giving up on us."

Abby smiled, leaning her head on his shoulder. "I never could," she said. "You're worth it. We're worth it."

For Abby and Jake, this season of renewal reminded them that a strong marriage doesn't happen by accident—it takes intentional effort, time, and prayer. They learned that even in the busiest seasons of life, making their relationship a priority was one of the best gifts they could give to each other and their family. With God's help, they were rebuilding their marriage and creating a deeper, richer connection than they had ever known.

"Though one may be overpowered, two can defend themselves. A cord of three strands is not quickly broken." – Ecclesiastes 4:12 (NIV)

> By prioritizing small but significant steps—like open communication, shared time, and prayer—we invite God to strengthen our bond and restore what feels lost.

This verse emphasizes the strength and resilience found in partnership, particularly within the marriage covenant. It highlights the power of unity in overcoming challenges and achieving greater stability. When two people unite in mutual support, their combined efforts create a foundation of strength. However, the true depth of this verse lies in the "third strand"—God's presence—which transforms the marriage from a human partnership into a divine covenant that is far stronger than either individual could achieve alone.

Not every marriage feels unified in every season, and not every husband is ready to focus on rebuilding the relationship. This can be a painful reality for wives who feel lonely or deserted. If you find yourself in this place, take comfort in knowing God sees you. He hears your prayers and understands the ache in your heart. While you may feel the weight of carrying the relationship, God is near, ready to strengthen and sustain you. Trust that He is working in ways you cannot yet see.

God's presence, the "third strand," offers hope and renewal for all couples. Abby and Jake's story reminds us that marriage requires intentionality and is not something we navigate alone. By prioritizing small but significant steps— like open communication, shared time, and prayer—we invite God to strengthen our bond and restore what feels lost.

This verse also serves as a reminder that marriage is a sacred covenant designed by God. It calls couples to protect and nurture their bond, not as two individuals coexisting, but as a unified team strengthened by their shared faith. This verse offers hope for Abby and Jake—and all couples— that no matter the challenges, a marriage built with God at the center can withstand trials and grow stronger over time. It becomes a living testimony of God's love and ability to sustain and bless those who trust Him.

REFLECTION:

1. Are we making time to nurture our marriage, or are other things taking priority?

What specific distractions or routines might be pulling us apart? How can I intentionally create space to reconnect and prioritize our relationship in our daily lives?

2. How can I remind him (and myself) that our marriage is a partnership centered on God?

Am I actively seeking God's guidance for our marriage and modeling reliance on Him? How can I encourage my husband to join me in inviting God into our relationship through prayer and shared faith?

3. What specific aspects of our marriage should I pray over today?

Are there areas where we need healing, restoration, or growth? How can I intercede for God's wisdom, grace, and blessing over our partnership?

PRAYER:

"Lord, thank You for the gift of marriage. Help me keep You at the center, strengthening us as a couple even when we feel distant or overwhelmed. When my husband is not ready to prioritize our relationship, remind me that You are still at work. Give me the patience and wisdom to love him well, and let my actions reflect Your grace and faithfulness. Strengthen our bond and renew our connection so that our marriage can be a testimony of Your love and a source of joy for our family. Amen."

TODAY'S CALL TO ACTION:

Spend 10 minutes with your husband today reflecting on a shared memory or dream. Pray together, asking God to strengthen your marriage and keep Him at the center.

Day 19

MY ROLE AS WIFE

"She does him good..."

Karen had always been a go-getter. She made to-do lists for her to-do lists, and she thrived on organization and efficiency. Her husband, Tom, was her complete opposite—laid-back, thoughtful, and deliberate in everything he did. While Karen loved these qualities in Tom, they sometimes frustrated her. When he took too long to make a decision or hesitated before tackling a task, Karen often found herself stepping in and taking over.

Over time, Karen began noticing how her behavior affected their marriage. Tom had started pulling back, offering his opinions less frequently and leaving more and more decisions to her. At first, Karen thought she was "just helping," but deep down, she knew she wasn't giving Tom the space to lead in their relationship. She often found herself questioning, Why can't he step up? Why do I always have to take the reins?

One evening, after a particularly tense discussion about their family budget, Karen sat alone in the living room, reflecting on their dynamic. She realized that while she longed for Tom to take the lead, she wasn't giving him room to do so. Her constant need to control every detail had created an unintentional competition in their marriage—a battle for who would make the final call. She prayed, "Lord, help me to be the wife Tom needs. Please show me how to encourage him instead of competing with him. Help me trust You and trust him more."

The following day, Karen decided to take a different approach. Instead of starting her usual monthly budget spreadsheet, she handed Tom the laptop and said, "Hey, I was thinking it might be better if you took the lead on this. I trust you to create a plan, and I'm here if you want to talk through anything."

Tom looked at her, surprised. "You're serious?" he asked, raising an eyebrow.

Karen smiled. "I'm serious. You're smart and capable, and I know you can handle this."

Over the next few days, Karen bit her tongue whenever she felt the urge to "correct" Tom's decisions. It wasn't easy—especially when he took a different approach than she would have—but she kept reminding herself of her prayer. Slowly, she began to see a change in Tom. He seemed more confident and more willing to share his ideas and opinions.

One evening, he surprised her by presenting a detailed budget plan that covered their expenses and included a strategy for saving for a family vacation. Karen was impressed. "This is amazing," she said, genuinely excited. "You've thought of everything."

Tom smiled, his eyes lighting up. "Thanks. It felt good to take this on."

Encouraged by this small victory, Karen continued to step back and let Tom take the lead in other areas. She also consciously made an effort to affirm him, pointing out his strengths and thanking him for his contributions. One weekend, as Tom tackled a long-overdue home improvement project, Karen brought him a cold drink and said, "I really appreciate how hard you work for our family. You're a great provider, and it means so much to me."

Tom paused, looking at her with genuine gratitude. "That means a lot to hear, Karen. I've always wanted to do my best for you and the kids, but sometimes I feel like I don't measure up."

Karen felt a lump rise in her throat. "You do more than measure up," she said. "And I'm sorry if I've made you feel otherwise. I want to be your biggest supporter, not someone who makes you doubt yourself."

That conversation was a turning point for both of them. Karen began to see her role as a wife not as someone who needed to "fix" or "control" but as someone who could build Tom up and empower him to be the leader God had called him to be. She realized that encouragement wasn't always about agreeing or staying silent—it was about trusting Tom, valuing his perspective, and creating an environment where he could thrive.

Over time, their marriage began to flourish in new ways. Tom stepped into his role more confidently, making decisions with thoughtfulness and care. Karen felt lighter, no longer burdened by the need to control everything. And together, they became a stronger team, united by trust and mutual respect.

Lisa Bevere once said, "Marriage was never meant to be a power struggle, it was meant to be a power union."

For Karen, this journey reminded her that her role wasn't to compete with Tom but to complement him—to encourage his leadership and trust God's plan for their marriage. For Tom, it was a lesson in how much he needed Karen's support and affirmation to become the man God had called him to be.

"She does him good, and not harm, all the days of her life." – Proverbs 31:12 (ESV)

This verse highlights the heart of a godly wife's role in marriage: to consistently do good to her husband, supporting and encouraging him in every season. It calls wives to be a source of strength, respect, and affirmation, fostering an environment where their husband can thrive. Rather than competing or criticizing, this verse emphasizes the importance of building him up with words and actions reflecting God's love and grace.

In the story, Karen's struggle to let go of control reveals a familiar dynamic in many marriages. Her tendency to take over or criticize stems from a desire for things to be done her way, which unintentionally undermines Tom's confidence and role as a leader in their home. This verse challenges Karen—and all wives—to shift their perspective and approach their husbands with the desire to do good, not harm. For Karen, this means stepping back, affirming Tom's abilities, and trusting God to equip him in his role.

The application of this verse is transformational for marriage. It invites wives to consider how their words and actions impact their husbands. Are they encouraging and affirming, or do they unintentionally wound or discourage? Doing good to one's husband involves being his cheerleader, supporting his decisions, and partnering with him to strengthen the marriage. It also means extending grace when he falls short, recognizing that marriage is a growth journey for both partners.

For Karen, embracing this principle transforms her marriage. When she begins to affirm Tom's strengths and entrust responsibilities to him, she sees him step into his role with greater confidence. This encourages a healthier dynamic where both spouses can contribute to the marriage without competition or resentment. Her decision to do him good creates a ripple effect, strengthening their partnership and fostering trust.

This verse also challenges wives to pray for their husbands, seeking God's guidance for ways to encourage them. By doing good "all the days of her life," a wife creates a legacy of faithfulness and love that not only blesses her husband but also honors God.

> **Trust that God's timing is perfect, and He can work in ways beyond what we can see or imagine.**

The journey can sometimes feel lonely for wives whose husbands may not share their faith. But know that God is with you, walking alongside you in prayer and patience. Your quiet example of love, grace, and faith can be a powerful witness, reflecting Christ's light in your marriage. Trust that God's timing is perfect, and He can work in ways beyond what we can see or imagine.

Ultimately, this verse reminds wives that their role is not about control but companionship and support. When wives seek to do good to their husbands through their words, actions, and prayers, they reflect God's heart for marriage, creating a partnership rooted in love, respect, and unity. For Karen and all wives, this verse is a call to be a source of strength and encouragement, helping their husbands thrive in their God-given roles while building a marriage that honors Christ.

Wife, your words will either be the bricks that build him up or the hammer that breaks him down. You get to choose. Choose wisely.

REFLECTION:

1. Do I tend to compete with him or try to control things in our marriage?

Are there specific situations where I struggle to relinquish control or trust his leadership? How can I surrender these tendencies to God and align my heart with His design for our partnership?

2. Are there ways I need to grow in trusting God's design for marriage?

Do I recognize areas where fear, pride, or insecurity may shape my approach to our partnership? How can I pray for God to transform my heart and help me embrace humility, grace, and faith in His plan for our relationship?

3. How can I pray for a heart that values harmony over control in our relationship?

What specific habits or attitudes in myself could I bring to God in prayer for transformation? How can I ask God to help me reflect humility, respect, and love in my role as his wife?

PRAYER:

"Father, thank You for the gift of marriage and the privilege of being my husband's partner in this life. Help me to be a source of encouragement and strength for him, reflecting Your love through my words and actions. Teach me to trust Your design for marriage and to release any need for control or competition that hinders our unity. Shape my heart to be a heart of humility, grace, and respect, and guide me in building him up to thrive in the role You have called him to. Remind me daily to lean on You for wisdom, patience, and love as we grow together. Lord, let our marriage be a reflection of Your goodness and a testimony of Your faithfulness. Amen."

TODAY'S CALL TO ACTION:

Reflect on an area where you may be competing or trying to control. Surrender that to God in prayer, and take a small step today to affirm your husband's leadership instead.

Day 20

~~~

RELATIONSHIP WITH THE HOLY SPIRIT

"But the Advocate...will remind you..."

Sarah had always admired her husband, Ben, for his steady faith. He attended church regularly, prayed with their family at mealtimes, and occasionally joined a men's Bible study. But deep down, Sarah sensed that something was missing. While Ben loved God and tried to live a good life, his relationship with the Holy Spirit felt distant and impersonal. He often relied on his own strength to navigate challenges, and Sarah could see how that was wearing him down.

Sarah's journey with the Holy Spirit had been transformative. She remembered how, years ago, she had struggled with fear and insecurity until she surrendered her heart to the Spirit's guidance and peace. It wasn't an overnight change, but over time, she had learned to lean into the Spirit for wisdom, courage, and strength. Now, seeing Ben wrestle with similar struggles, she longed for him to experience the same intimacy with God. But she knew she couldn't force it. All she could do was pray.

One evening, after a particularly stressful day at work, Ben came home exhausted. "Everything feels like a battle," he admitted over dinner. "I try so hard to do the right thing, but it feels like I'm always falling short. I don't know how much more I can handle."

Sarah reached for his hand, her heart aching for him. "Ben, you don't have to carry it all on your own," she said gently. "Have you ever thought about asking the Holy Spirit for help? He's there to guide you, to give you wisdom and strength when you feel like you're at the end of yourself."

Ben looked at her, his brow furrowed. "I don't know," he said. "I've always felt like God gave us what we needed to figure things out. Isn't relying on the Holy Spirit just asking for an easy way out?"

Sarah smiled softly, shaking her head. "It's not about taking the easy way out, Ben. It's about walking with Him. The Spirit isn't just there to solve problems—He's there to guide us, to remind us of God's love, and to help us live in His power instead of our own. I've seen what happens when I try to do it all myself, and it's exhausting. But when I lean into the Spirit, there's a peace and strength that I can't explain."

Ben didn't respond immediately, but Sarah could tell her words had struck a chord. That night, as she lay in bed, she prayed for him. "Lord, draw Ben closer to You. Help him to see that Your Spirit is not a crutch but a gift. Let him experience the fullness of Your presence and know that he's never alone."

A few days later, Ben surprised Sarah by asking if she wanted to pray with him. "I've been thinking about what you said," he admitted. "Maybe I need to stop trying to figure everything out alone and begin to ask God to guide me more."

Together, they knelt in their living room. Sarah listened as Ben prayed a simple but heartfelt prayer: "Lord, I've been trying to handle everything myself, and I'm tired. I need Your help. Show me how to trust You and let Your Spirit lead me. I don't want to do this alone anymore."

Over the following weeks, Sarah began to see subtle but profound changes in Ben. He started praying more and reading his Bible, not out of obligation but because he wanted to. He began talking about how he felt the Spirit nudging him. Whether to encourage a coworker, step out in faith at church, or let go of his worries. One Sunday, as they walked out of church together, Ben turned to Sarah and said, "I've been asking the Spirit to guide me more. I feel like I'm finally starting to understand what that means. It's like I'm not carrying everything alone anymore."

Sarah's eyes filled with tears as she nodded. "That's the beauty of it," she said. "You were never meant to carry it all."

Ben's renewed relationship with the Holy Spirit didn't just impact him—it transformed their entire family. Their kids noticed how much calmer and more present he seemed, and they began asking him questions about faith. His coworkers commented on the peace he carried, even amid challenges. It was a joy for Sarah to watch Ben grow deeper in his faith, walking in step with the Spirit and allowing God to lead him in every area of his life.

For Sarah and Ben, this journey was a reminder that a relationship with the Holy Spirit isn't about perfection or having all the answers—it's about daily surrender, trusting God to lead, and allowing His power to work in and through us. Together, they learned that walking with the Spirit brought peace and the strength and purpose they had been longing for all along.

"But the Advocate, the Holy Spirit, whom the Father will send in my name, will teach you all things and will remind you of everything I have said to you." – John 14:26 (NIV)

This verse emphasizes the critical role of the Holy Spirit as our Advocate, Teacher, and Helper. Jesus promised His disciples that the Holy Spirit would guide them into truth, remind them of His teachings, and equip them for life's challenges. For believers today, the Holy Spirit is an ever-present source of wisdom, comfort, and strength, empowering us to live in alignment with God's will.

Ben's struggle to rely on the Holy Spirit reflects a common issue many Christians face—trying to navigate life in their own strength rather than leaning on God's Spirit. His frustration and feelings of inadequacy stem from forgetting that the Holy Spirit is available and actively working to guide and equip him. This verse reassures Ben that he doesn't have to face his struggles alone; the Holy Spirit is there to teach, strengthen, and remind him of God's promises.

The application of this verse challenges all believers to culti- vate an intentional relationship with the Holy Spirit. This involves inviting the Spirit into every aspect of our lives, whether decision-making, navigating relationships, or handling stress and uncertainty. The Holy Spirit brings clarity when we're confused, peace when we're anxious, and courage when we feel weak. Turning to Him allows God's wisdom and strength to flow through us, transforming our lives and enabling us to reflect Christ to others.

> The Holy Spirit is an ever-present source of wisdom, comfort, and strength, empowering us to live in alignment with God's will.

Learning to pray and ask for the Spirit's guidance is a turning point for Ben. As he begins to rely on the Spirit, he experiences practical help in daily challenges and a more profound sense of God's presence and peace. His openness to the Spirit's leading positively impacts his relationship with Sarah and their family as he begins to live with greater inten- tionality and faith.

This verse also reminds believers of the Spirit's role in helping us remember and apply God's Word. Through the Spirit, scripture comes alive in our hearts, providing the wisdom and encouragement we need to walk in obedience. The Spirit doesn't just reveal the truth but empowers us to live it out, even when it's difficult.

Ultimately, this verse calls believers to move beyond a surface-level faith into a dynamic, Spirit-led relationship with God. For Ben and all of us, building this relationship requires surrender, trust, and a willingness to listen to the Spirit's promptings. When we do, we experience a life that is not only guided by God's wisdom but also filled with His peace, purpose, and power. Through the Holy Spirit, we are equipped to glorify God in all that we do, becoming living testimonies of His grace and love.

If your husband does not yet have a relationship with the Holy Spirit, pray for his heart to be softened and open to God's presence. Even if he is not ready to seek spiritual growth, your walk with the Spirit can bring peace and light into your marriage.

REFLECTION:

1. How can I pray that my husband grows in his relationship with the Holy Spirit?

Am I lifting up specific areas of his life where he needs guidance, wisdom, or peace? How can I ask God to help him hear and respond to the Spirit's promptings with clarity and trust?

2. Do I see evidence of the Spirit's work in his life, and do I affirm it?

Am I attentive to the moments when he displays Spirit-led wisdom, patience, or courage? How can I affirm and encourage him to continue leaning on the Holy Spirit in his daily walk?

3. What steps can I take to create a home environment that nurtures spiritual growth for both of us?

Are there habits, like praying together or sharing scripture, that we can incorporate to invite the Spirit into our home? How can I foster an atmosphere that supports both of us in seeking God's presence and direction?

PRAYER:

"Holy Spirit, I come to You with a heart full of gratitude and hope. Thank You for walking with us through this prayer journey and for Your constant presence in our lives. I lift up my husband to You, asking that You fill his heart with Your wisdom, peace, and guidance. Remind him daily that he is never alone and that Your strength is available to him in every challenge and decision he faces.

Holy Spirit, soften his heart to Your voice and lead him into a deeper relationship with You. Help him trust Your prompting

and seek Your presence in all areas of his life—his work, relationships, and personal growth. Let him experience the joy
and freedom that result from walking in step with You.
I also ask that You work in my own heart. Teach me to be
patient, to love steadfastly, and to trust in Your perfect
timing. Let my life reflect Your peace and grace, a light that
draws my husband closer to You. Together, help us create a
home where Your presence is welcome, faith is nurtured, and
love flourishes.

As I close this prayer journey, I commit our marriage and
family to You. May we always lean on Your strength and
wisdom, allowing You to guide us as we grow in faith and
unity. Let our lives glorify You and testify to Your transformative power. Thank You for being our Advocate, our Teacher,
and our Comforter. I trust You, Holy Spirit, to continue to lead
us in love, purpose, and joy. Amen."

TODAY'S CALL TO ACTION:

Pray for your husband to experience the Holy Spirit's presence in a tangible way. If he's open, suggest praying
together, inviting the Spirit to guide and refresh both of you.

Summary

A CELEBRATION OF PRAYERFUL PARTNERSHIP

No two marriages are the same, and no two husbands are on the same journey. Whether your husband is thriving, struggling, or somewhere in between, God's grace is sufficient for both of you. He has uniquely equipped you to love, pray, and support your husband in ways that reflect His perfect design for your marriage. Trust that His plans are always for good, even when the path feels unclear.

If your husband hesitates to lead or struggles with spiritual growth, remember that this is not a reflection of his worth or potential. It may stem from deeper fears or doubts, and God is more than able to meet him there. As a wife, your role is not to push or control but to love and support him, inviting God to work in ways beyond your ability. You become a partner in God's divine work in his heart through your prayers and encouragement.

This journey has been about partnering with God in

prayer—whether your husband is flourishing as a leader or facing challenges. God's love meets us exactly where we are, and your prayerfulness becomes a powerful testimony of His grace. Prayer isn't about immediate results but about trusting God's sovereignty. Whether or not you see changes right away, your prayers are sowing seeds that He will nurture in His perfect timing. Keep lifting your husband up, knowing God's love and power are at work, even in the unseen moments.

When progress feels slow, or setbacks arise, take heart: God is not finished with your marriage—or your husband. His work often unfolds in the quiet, hidden places of the heart. Lean into His promises, trusting that He is shaping both of you for His glory. Every prayer you've prayed has mattered, and every act of faithfulness has drawn you closer to the One who holds your marriage in His hands.

The journey can sometimes feel lonely for wives whose husbands may not share their faith. But God is with you, walking alongside you in prayer and patience. Your quiet example of love, grace, and faith can shine as a powerful witness, reflecting Christ's light in your marriage. Trust His timing, knowing that He is able to work in ways far beyond what you can imagine.

As you close this devotional, celebrate what God has done in your heart over these 20 days. Your prayers, reflections, and commitment to being a wife who seeks God have not gone unnoticed by Him. Whether your husband sees the fruit of your efforts now or later, your faithfulness is a beautiful act of love that mirrors God's faithfulness to you.

Take joy in knowing that God is not only working in your husband but in you as well. You are a praying wife, an encourager, and a source of strength in your marriage. Embrace the calling to love your husband with the patience, grace, and courage that only God can provide. He is faithful to complete the work He has begun in both of you. Step forward with hope and confidence, knowing that God's plans for your marriage are far greater than you can imagine. Keep praying, trusting, and loving—because He is with you through it all.

About the Author

Susan Halaut is the founder of The Cultivated Marriage and a dynamic speaker, coach, and trainer based in the hill country of Texas. She and her husband, Jeff, are *Married For A Purpose* Coaches who equip couples, especially those in blended families and those navigating life after active parenting, to build thriving, Christ-centered relationships. She loves sunny beach getaways, time with their four boys and their families, and playing with her dogs.

You pour your heart into your marriage, longing for your husband to step into his God-given role.

But what about you?

The Individual Reboot is your chance to refocus, aligning your thought life, faith, relationships, and purpose with God's design.

Gain clarity, set priorities, and walk boldly in His plan.

It's time to reset, refocus, and reclaim your calling!

To learn more about Susan and how to get started with your own Individual Reboot, visit:

SusanHalaut.com

www.ingramcontent.com/pod-product-compliance
Lightning Source LLC
Chambersburg PA
CBHW062105080426
42734CB00012B/2762